THE SENECA ARMY ★ DEPOT

FIGHTING WARS FROM THE NEW YORK HOME FRONT

WALTER GABLE
& CAROLYN ZOGG

THE
History
PRESS

Published by The History Press
Charleston, SC 29403
www.historypress.net

First published 2012
Second printing 2013

Manufactured in the United States

ISBN 978.1.60949. 820.7

Library of Congress CIP data applied for.

Notice: The information in this book is true and complete to the best of our knowledge. It is offered without guarantee on the part of the authors or The History Press. The authors and The History Press disclaim all liability in connection with the use of this book.

CONTENTS

PREFACE

How ironic that Ken Burn's documentary *The War* is being rebroadcast by Public Television just as this book readies for press. Scenes and news clips of German submarines in New York Harbor, its city residents uncooperative with the government-requested blackouts—This was the scene in 1941, before Pearl Harbor, when not many upstaters, including Seneca County farmers, took notice of Nazi and Japanese aggression coming to their land. Communication was slow, and survival of the Great Depression was the order of the day.

Watching *The War* unfold makes me take another look at *Seneca Army Depot*, the text that Walt and I are producing. How does 11,000 acres of farmland come to be earmarked for a munitions depot, confiscated by the Department of War with such speed and swiftness that it produced its own war-like destruction? Citizens, led to believe in their country's patriotism, had to cooperate and leave their ancestral homes and land. Bulldozers took over, flattening houses and barns and trees and flowering shrubs. Burning was everywhere, similar to General Sullivan's routing of the American Indians, through the same lands, destroying people and peach trees. Did the government know it desperately needed to prepare for war, quickly, yet in secrecy? Had it known its citizens would not believe war was coming across the Atlantic, the Pacific?

This book is a little-known story of how and why government action changed the fabric of a land and its people. A land long-known for its ability to change the world, with the Women's Rights Movement,

Note the location of Seneca County within New York State. *Courtesy of Michael Karpovage.*

the beginning of Mormonism, the Underground Railroad, the Vote for Women.

It is my hope that making this small piece of history, researched and written by Walt Gable, available for anyone to read or listen to, will make us think of our government and its actions, how our government affects us every day, how we act or react.

In Seneca Falls, New York, 1997, Ken Burns was filming *Not for Ourselves Alone,* the story of Elizabeth Cady Stanton and Susan B. Anthony. He was asked to speak with a number of 4th graders gathered at the Stanton House about his work. He ended his remarks by saying, "Our past is our greatest teacher." May our past be our greatest teacher as we learn more of what was happening in our backyard in the years between 1941 and 2011. May we think that those who follow will gather insight and learn from our past.

—Carolyn Zogg

INTRODUCTION

From World War II through Project Desert Storm, the Seneca Army Depot in mid-Seneca County, New York, was a major supply base for the army. It had been established by the War Department in 1941 to help provide defense against possible enemy attack of the northeast Atlantic coast. As quickly as possible, a few hundred munitions storage igloos were constructed. Following formal United States entry into World War II, the work of the Seneca Ordnance Depot (its original name until August 1962 when it was changed officially to the Seneca Army Depot) expanded into being a major supply and storage facility. At the end of that war, this depot continued in that role. It also became a major facility for IPE—industrial plant equipment maintenance. Starting in the mid-1950s, the depot took on an additional role—storage of "special weapons"—in its North Depot Activity. In 1983, the depot carried on its work throughout a summer and fall marked by anti-nuclear weapons demonstrations that were reported nationwide. The demise of the Cold War led to the end of storage of "special weapons" at this depot. Following that downsizing in operations, the Seneca Army Depot was formally closed as an active base in 2000.

In November 2010, a group of local historians meeting with Seneca County Historian Walter Gable decided they wanted to do something in 2011 to mark the seventieth anniversary of the establishment of the depot in 1941. A three-part series of public programs was presented. Much research was done for these presentations. Over twenty individuals were

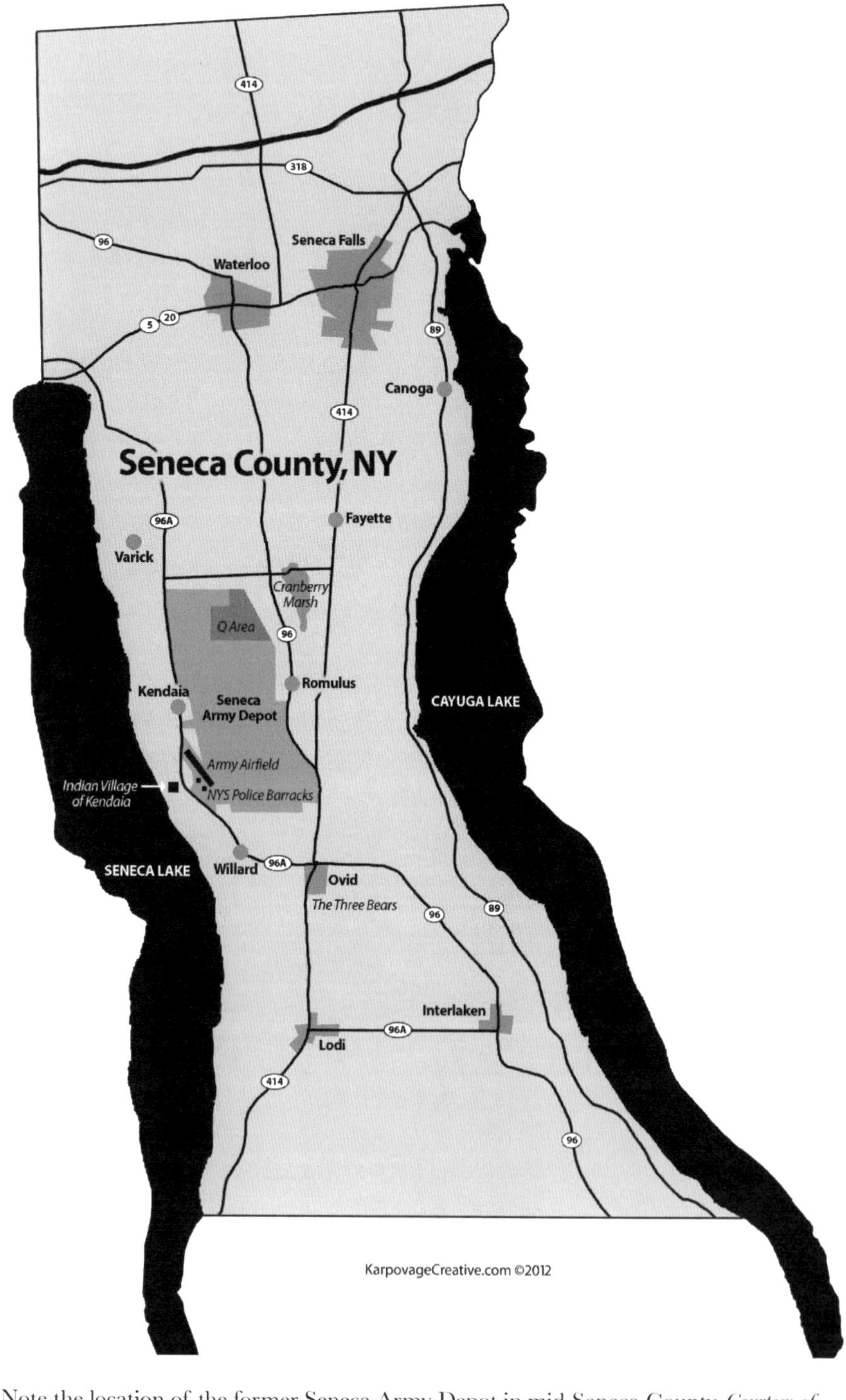

Note the location of the former Seneca Army Depot in mid-Seneca County. *Courtesy of Michael Karpovage.*

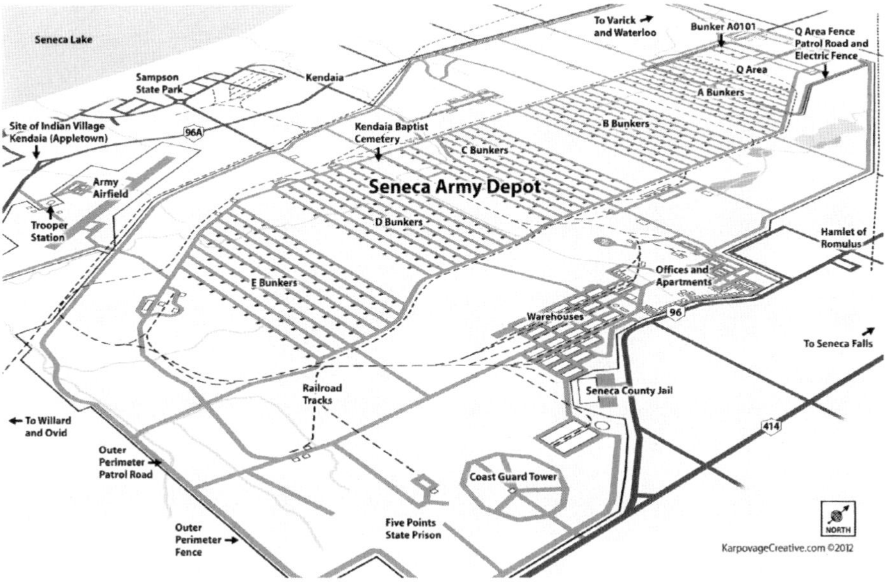

Note the location of the munitions igloos of the depot, the Q area where the "special weapons" activity took place, as well as the location of new operations on the former depot. *Courtesy of Michael Karpovage.*

interviewed. The group of local historians decided that we had gathered so much information that we needed to publish a book. The information presented in this book tells much of the "big picture" of the story of the former Seneca Army Depot, some of which many local residents had very little specific knowledge. Even more importantly, through the interviews conducted, we get some real insights into both the day-to-day operations of this military facility and the profound role of this supply base.

The seventieth anniversary of the establishment of the Seneca Army Depot was celebrated in other ways, thanks to the work of this group of local historians. One of these was a visit to the cemetery of the First Baptist Church of Romulus (locals refer to the church as the Kendaia Baptist Church) on the former depot property. When the War Department forced property owners—including that church—to sell their properties to make way for the Seneca Ordnance Depot, it promised that this cemetery would be preserved and that people would continue to have access to it. For years, the public has been allowed to visit the cemetery on the Sunday of Memorial Day weekend. So, on May 29, 2011, the group of local historians placed a wreath at the cemetery. In his

Several individuals and organizations donated the funds for this historic marker to honor the families that were dispossessed from their properties. *Courtesy of Walter Gable.*

The Seneca County Board of Supervisors paid for this historic marker denoting the years and activities of the Seneca Army Depot. *Courtesy of Walter Gable.*

brief remarks, Gable pointed out how the federal government has kept its promise about the continued existence of this cemetery.

Another part of the seventieth anniversary celebration was the erection of two historic markers. On July 12, 2012, there was a formal dedication of a historic marker honoring the dispossessed families. That marker also honors those families that were dispossessed from their properties to make way for the Sampson Naval Training Station in 1942. At that ceremony, a few members of the dispossessed families were present. The keynote speaker at that dedication was Dean Bruno, who wrote a master's thesis dealing with these dispossessed families. In that thesis, he pointed out the dishonor of these families never having been properly recognized for their sacrifice. In October 2012, another historic marker was dedicated to denote the years and activities of the former Seneca Army Depot. These historic markers, along with this book, help to tell the story of the Seneca Army Depot. It is a story that shows how much of the United States' ability to fight in several overseas wars was made possible because of the efforts of workers at the Seneca Army Depot.

—Walter Gable

CHAPTER 1
A HISTORY OF THE AREA

Prior to the American Revolution

Probably the earliest known humans to reside in this area were the people of the so-called Lamoka culture. Between approximately 3500 and 1300 BC, these people were primarily hunters, fishers and gatherers.[1]

Later there were the Algonquian Indians. Still later there were the Indians of the Iroquois Confederation, especially the Senecas and the Cayugas.

The first Europeans to meet with Indians of the Finger Lakes area were missionaries. In 1656, a group of Jesuits visited the Cayugas and established a mission near Savannah. In 1750, two Moravian missionaries, Cammerhoff and Zeisberger, visited the Cayugas on their way westward to meet with the Senecas. Reverend Samuel Kirkland visited the area in 1765 and resided with the Senecas for more than a year.[2]

The Sullivan Expedition of 1779

In the first six months of the American Revolution, the Six Nations of the Iroquois were officially neutral in the conflict. In early 1777, the Iroquois agreed to a British request that they participate in the conflict on the British side. During the summer and fall of 1777, the Iroquois conducted several raiding parties on colonials and actively helped the British in two major military engagements at Oriskany and Wyoming. In the spring of 1778, Iroquois under Chief Joseph Brant attacked Cobleskill and conducted raids in the Mohawk Valley. The next spring, they joined with the upper Susquehanna Indians to burn European settlements between the Mohawk River and the Delaware River.[3]

In 1779, General Washington ordered the Sullivan Expedition to put a stop to the aid the Iroquois Indians were giving to the British during the American Revolution. In a letter to Major General Horatio Gates (who declined to head up this task), General Washington stated the purpose of the expedition was "to carry the war into the heart of the country of the Six Nations, to cut off their settlements, destroy next year's crops, and do them every other mischief, which time and circumstance would permit."[4] Washington then named Major General John Sullivan to head up the expedition, and instructed him to wage a "scorched earth" campaign. Between September 4 and 5, 1799, several of the troops of the Sullivan Expedition arrived and camped at the Seneca Indians' settlement at Kendaia. Lieutenant Colonel Adam Hurley recorded that the village was "situated on a rising ground, in the midst of an extensive apple and peach orchard, within a half a mile of the lake [Seneca]." The Indians residing at this Kendaia village had fled before the arrival of the troops.[5] The Sullivan forces found, however, a white man named Luke Swetland who had been captured along with Joseph Blanchard at Nanticoke, Pennsylvania, on August 24, 1778, and taken to Kendaia. In the little over a year that he had been there at Kendaia, he had been given to an old squaw who kept him as her son. He had been employed in the making of salt some twenty miles from Kendaia, probably at Watkins Glen. Swetland said that about five hundred male Indians and about three hundred Tories fled from Kendaia two days before Sullivan forces arrived.[6]

In his journal entry, Ensign Daniel Gookin described "a number of 200 old apple trees and peach trees plenty."[7] The troops destroyed approximately twenty longhouses as well as several large fields of corn and girdled many of the fruit trees.[8] Shortly after departing Kendaia, as the Sullivan forces proceeded to Kanadasaga (present-day Geneva), Major Jeremiah Fogg, in a journal entry dated September 7, 1779, described his vision for whites to settle this area: "The land between the Seneca and Cayuga lakes appears good, level, and well timbered; affording a sufficiency for twenty elegant townships, which in process of time will doubtless add to the importance of America."[9] All in all, this Sullivan Expedition destroyed some forty Iroquois villages, an estimated 160,000 bushels of corn as well as killing many fruit trees. In the process, many soldiers gained a first-hand vision of the tremendous economic opportunity for white settlers in this area.[10]

Early White Settlement

After the American Revolution, the area was part of the military tract that was divided into lots to be given as bounty lands for New York soldiers and officers who had served in the Revolutionary War. This did not actually take place for several years following the end of the war for some key reasons. First, it took time for negotiating a lengthy series of peace treaties with the Iroquois. Second, a territory dispute between New York and Massachusetts over the western frontier lands was not resolved until the Treaty of Hartford in 1786. Then the lands of the new military tract had to be surveyed into a series of townships of sixty thousand acres that could be further divided into one hundred lots of six hundred acres each. The actual assigning of lots to the war veterans did not begin until 1790. It is estimated that fewer than two hundred of the original eligible soldiers actually settled on the land they received from the military bounty. Some had died in the eleven years that had passed. Some had settled elsewhere in this military tract. Many of the lots were eventually sold to speculators and middlemen, who then advertised the land to potential buyers throughout the new nation.[11] More specifically, only three or possibly four of the soldiers actually settled on the lot they received in what became Seneca County.[12]

The approximate 11,500 acres of the Seneca Ordnance Depot were located in the towns of Romulus and Varick (which was created out of part of the Romulus town in 1830). More specifically, the depot included these lots:

- Varick
    1. portions of Lot 51, 52, 53, 58 and 63
    2. all of Lot 56, 57, 61 and 62

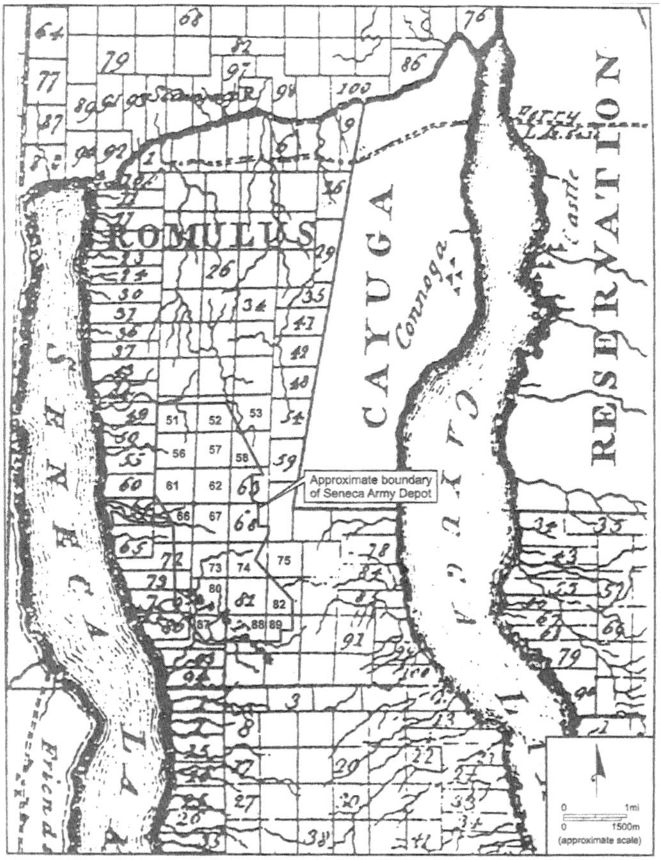

Note the numbered lots of the Military Tract of the towns of Romulus and Varick that became the Seneca Ordnance Depot in 1941. *Courtesy of the Seneca County Historian's Office.*

- Romulus
  1. portions of Lot 64, 66, 68,72, 74, 75, 79, 82, 86, 87, 88, and 89
  2. all of Lot 67, 73, 80, and 81[13]

THE AREA FROM 1794 TO 1941

The town of Romulus had been established in 1794, when the present Seneca County was part of Onondaga County (prior to that the area had been part of Herkimer County and even earlier it had been part of Montgomery County). At that time, the town of Romulus extended all the way north to Lake Ontario. In 1800, the portion of Romulus that was just south of the Seneca River became the town of Washington (present-day town of Fayette). In 1830, the remaining northern portion of the town of Romulus became the town of Varick. On March 24, 1804, Seneca County was created out of the western portion of Cayuga County (which had been created out of the western portion of Onondaga County in 1799).

In early Seneca County, European settlers tended to be subsistence farmers. As a system of land and water transportation routes developed—the Great Genesee Road and, especially, the canal on the Seneca River (circa 1818) and its connection with the Erie Canal (1828)—extensive markets opened up for the grains and fruits that could be produced in Seneca County and the rest of the Finger Lakes area. Later, the railroads would prove to be an even better means of transportation of agricultural products from Seneca County to markets in the New York City metropolitan area.

By 1850, the preponderance of the present depot tract was occupied by farms. The average farm located on depot land in 1850 had a value of approximately $3,000. In addition to farms, the depot land contained scattered other land uses in the mid-nineteenth century. These land uses generally served the farms and farmers and included blacksmith shops, cemeteries, a sawmill, a wheelwright's shop, a cider mill and a warehouse. This warehouse was owned by Daniel Cooley and was located on the eastern shore of Seneca Lake. It was used to store goods that had been or were being shipped along the lake.[14]

By 1880, the amount of land in the county devoted to farming increased to 204,258 acres (compared to 150,357 acres in 1860). In the second half of the nineteenth century, the Finger Lakes wine industry expanded rapidly. As this winemaking grew, Romulus became a grape growing and shipping area. In 1889, the Seneca Lake Niagara Vineyard was founded. It had 255 acres of vineyards with Charles Smith supervising fifty-five workers. In 1895, that vineyard shipped about five hundred tons of grapes from the Romulus Depot. By 1895, some 6,000 acres of land in Seneca County were devoted to raising grapes. Varick town had 544 of these acres, and Romulus town had 318 acres.[15] In the harvest of 1926, some forty-five railroad cars full of grapes were loaded and shipped from the Romulus station.[16]

Also, late in the nineteenth century, dairy farming increased in importance in Seneca County. M.J. Briggs organized creameries at Hayts Corners in Romulus, Bearytown (present Fayette) in Varick and Farmer (present Interlaken) in Covert. These creameries received about 3,500; 4,000; and 5,000 pounds of milk daily, respectively.[17]

In 1920, Seneca County had approximately 160,296 acres of farmland. Over 87 percent of the land area of the county was farmland. About two-thirds of the farms in the county were owner-operated. The total value of all crops produced was $5,963,520. A total of 52,542 acres of farmland was devoted to cereal production, mainly corn, oats and wheat. There were 253,433 fruit trees, of which 131,784 were apple trees and 45,439 were peach trees. A total of 3,804,595 pounds of grapes were harvested from 466,752 bearing vines.[18]

While the majority of the land area of what became the depot consisted of farms, there were other noteworthy uses. Two churches and three country schools were located on what became depot land. The First Baptist Church of Romulus (near the hamlet of Kendaia and commonly referred to as the Kendaia Baptist Church) was founded in 1795. In October 1941, the church site was sold to the federal government. Its adjacent cemetery was retained and was included in the grounds of the depot. The church building was bought, dismantled and removed to Irelandville near Watkins Glen. The Wesleyan Methodist church was built in 1878. The country schools included the McLafferty School (Romulus District #7), Sutton School (Romulus District #6) and Kendaia School (Romulus District #8).[19]

In the summer of 1941, the federal government acquired over 150 parcels for the Seneca Ordnance Depot. By September 1941, the dispossessed farm families had been relocated.[20]

CHAPTER 2
WHY THE SENECA COUNTY SITE

BACKGROUND

World War II was the largest and most violent armed conflict in the history of mankind. However, the more than sixty-five years that now separates us from that conflict at the writing of this book has exacted its toll on our collective knowledge. While World War II continues to absorb the interest of military scholars and historians, as well as its veterans, young Americans have grown to maturity largely unaware of the political, social and military implications of a war that, more than any other, united us as a people with a common purpose.[21]

World War II broke out in Europe in September 1939. Although the United States did not formally enter the war until the Pearl Harbor attack of December 7, 1941, the Franklin D. Roosevelt administration was making active preparations for involvement in this war. From July 1, 1940 to December 1, 1941, the United States government spent $12.7 billion on national defense. This amount had increased rapidly from $199 million in July 1940 to $1.40 billion in November 1941.[22] These defense preparations included the establishment of four "munitions depots"—two for each coast—that could supply bombs for American aircraft protecting our coastal areas. The four munitions depots were at Umatilla, Oregon; Fort Wingate, New Mexico; Anniston, Alabama; and Seneca County, New York.[23]

THE BASIC REASONS FOR CHOOSING THIS SENECA COUNTY SITE

The Roosevelt administration needed to select a site for the basic protection of the east coast area from Washington, D.C., to Maine. Prior to naming Seneca County as the base site, the War Department evaluated approximately sixty possible locations throughout the northeastern United States. Three recommended locations were forwarded to a special committee of the army for final consideration. These sites were in Kentucky, Pennsylvania and Seneca County.[24] The Seneca County site was declared the winner for a number of key reasons:

- Two major rail lines bordered the seventeen-mile tract—this enhanced transportation and logistical operations. On the west

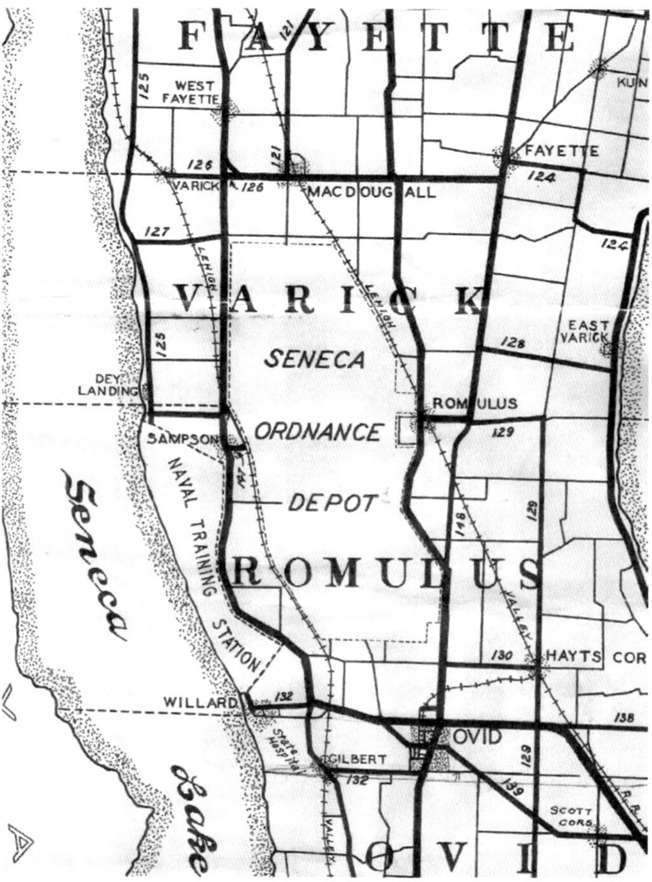

There were railroad lines on the east and west sides of the Seneca Ordnance Depot. Also shown is the Sampson Naval Training Station, established in 1942. *Courtesy of the Seneca County Historian's Office.*

side of what would become the Seneca Ordnance Depot was a branch of the Lehigh Valley Railroad, with a station at Kendaia. On the east side was the Geneva to Ithaca branch of the Lehigh Valley Railroad, with a station at Romulus.

- The lightly populated country provided a remote location far from any major metropolitan centers, while still within range to supply coastal defenses. In fact, all of the ten depots being erected by the federal government in 1941 were located at a distance from large centers of population.[25]

As early as July 18, 1941, an editorial in the *Waterloo Observer* pointed out that this might be good for the majority of the nation's population, but it would possibly be especially tough on the particular remote rural community chosen. Specifically, the editorial included this paragraph: "The location of such a huge project in a comparatively small county, mostly rural, has even greater effects than it would have in a larger county or in an area closer to a large center of population. Already it is beginning to change the lives, the thoughts, and plans of hundreds of people in this vicinity. Such speed of operation has not been witnessed here before. Such lavish expenditure of money is entirely new to both business men and laboring men here."[26]

"Asked why the depot was established in Seneca County, Major Gerald P. Botsford said he understood the storage dump for munitions was needed within two to three hundred miles of the Atlantic coast."[27] (Major G.F. Botsford was the executive officer, working under Colonel Paul B. Parker, for the construction project at the Seneca Ordnance Depot.)

- Just a few inches beneath the top soil was a layer of shale—this would absorb the shock from detonations, reducing the chances of catastrophic mishap in case a munitions bunker exploded.[28]

Colonel Paul B. Parker frequently told local community groups in 1941 that local residents didn't have to worry about the explosion of any munitions depot, unless there was an attack by foreign aircraft. He said, "An explosion probably would rattle windows in the area of the depot and there would be a ringing sensation in ears of those within range, but aside from that no danger exists."[29]

The *Syracuse Post-Standard* in a June 15, 1941 story had this to say about the shale:

> *Underneath, at from two to three feet on the average, is a heavy layer of shale which for more than a century has drained the pregnant soil. It is this layer of shale that residents believe caused the government to plant its new crop between the two shiny lakes. The ammunition will be buried in this shale in individual dumps. The loose, scaly rock would provide a cushion to absorb the shock of an explosion, preventing it from spreading over the entire 18 square miles. The talk of explosion, incidentally, is what troubles those on the outskirts of the area. What about their homes if one comes?*

- Compared to other locations on the list, land in Seneca County was cheap, allowing the federal government to reduce project cost.[30]
- The federal government perceived that the local residents were true patriots and were not likely to raise any significant protests. Colonel Paul B. Parker explained to one local group, "The all-American make up of the population of this county was one important factor in the choice of Seneca County as the site for this part of the national defense program."[31] At another time, Major Gerald P. Botsford, referred to the "preponderately good American stock," a fact "considered important from the point of sabotage."[32]
- Coupled with this was the fact that the local residents were perceived to be unable to mount any significant protest because there was no existing local mechanism to do so.[33]

Significantly, the price required to purchase the land in mid-Seneca County was expected to be about twice the normal value of the land. The selection committee, however, realized that this increased expense would be offset by the level nature of the site. The committee also was swayed by the fact that an airfield could be built if necessary on neighboring land. Reports that there would be less expressed opposition from the Seneca County residents than would be encountered with either the Kentucky or the Pennsylvania sites also must have played a role in the ultimate selection of the Seneca County site.[34]

Politics as a Possible Reason

In addition to these reasons, it is very possible that politics may have played an influential role in locating the depot in Seneca County. Much of the comment here is based on what Walter Gable was told by Miss Ethel Buckley, his high school history teacher.

Seneca Country residents were represented in the U.S. House of Representatives by John Taber of Auburn. Taber was the ranking Republican on the House Appropriations Committee and had acquired nicknames such as "Meat-Ax John" for the way he cut what he considered to be excess spending in the budgets of President Franklin D. Roosevelt. In January 1941, President Roosevelt presented Congress with a budget request of more than $17 billion, of which nearly $11 billion was marked for defense, including substantial funding for the Lend-Lease program. Taber, like many of his Republican colleagues, opposed the president's request and decried Roosevelt's thinly veiled efforts to bring the United States into the war. During the spring of 1941, Taber changed his position and threw his support behind Roosevelt's request. A few months later, the War Department named Seneca County as the location for the new depot. Was this more than just a coincidence? It could well have been possible that a deal had been struck between the president and the congressman—in return for his bipartisan support for the Roosevelt-desired appropriations for Lend-Lease, the president would see to it that one of the military munitions bases would be located in the congressman's district. Apparently no documented evidence of this exists, but it is possible that there was a quid pro quo kind of understanding. There were also obvious reasons as to why the congressman would not want to have any public record of such a deal or understanding—Taber would not want to have his name associated with the dispossession of more than 150 families from his home district.[35]

There is another piece to the possibility of politics playing a major role in the selection of a Seneca County site. The chairman of the Seneca County Democratic Party at the time was James Boyle, who lived on Willers Road in the town of Varick. According to Mrs. Charmion Dinsmore, one of Boyle's daughters, he can be given much of the credit for securing this site. He spent much time in Washington, D.C., and on the telephone actively working to get this site selected.[36]

A Buffalo newspaper in August 1941 put the reasons for the choice of site rather bluntly: "Adolf Hitler, the Army will tell you, is the cause of the uprooting taking place on this rural plateau…the United States is determined the enemy will not find out bases near the easily traversed sea and is erecting four inland depots, one here and others in the South, Southwest and Northwest. Planes guarding the Atlantic coast from Maine to Washington will load their bombs in Seneca County."[37]

CHAPTER 3
THE DISPOSSESSED FAMILIES

This chapter was written by Sally VanRiper Eller, who was born in Romulus, New York, just a few months after her parents were forced by the U.S. government to move from their Seneca County home in July 1941 to make way for the Seneca Ordnance Depot. Her maternal and paternal grandparents were also forced to abandon their farms as part of the 110 families that were dispossessed to make way for army preparations for World War II.

The smoke from burning homes, barns and crops was heavy on the day in July 1941 when my Uncle Wilford Lisk returned to his farm to retrieve his last possessions, including the only garden crop he planted that year, a few cucumber plants. The families who were forced to move from their farms that summer were given three days notice to move. But when my uncle returned on the second day for the rest of his belongings, the house and barns had been ransacked, despite guards posted by the U.S. Army. My uncle's daughter, Florence Vargason, recently told me that he was devastated to find that the cucumbers had been stolen. "That was the worst of the whole thing for him," Florence said. Also gone was the beloved lamp that had hung over their dining room table for decades.

Throughout my life, I heard stories of the ordeal and grief that were imposed on my parents, grandparents, aunts and uncles in the summer of 1941, just a few months before I was born. That summer, the U.S. government was gearing up for what seemed to be an inevitable war against the forces of Hitler in Europe, and the war machine came to the towns of Romulus and Varick where most of my family lived.

On the evening of June 10, 1941, the plans to establish the Seneca County Army Ordnance Depot were formally announced to residents crowded into the Romulus school auditorium. L.P. Walker of the War Department spoke at length about the need for sacrifice and the willingness of the people of Seneca County to do their part to secure the defenses of a most grateful nation. A hush fell over the audience as they realized that any that lived and farmed within the ten thousand acres would have to move out that summer.

Federal Munitions Depot Will Occupy 18 Square Miles South of Seneca Falls

> *The federal government, about July 1, will begin preparing the fruitful flatlands between Seneca and Cayuga lakes to receive a new crop—the sterile seeds of war.*
> *Where for more than 150 years these tabled* [sic] *acres have yielded an abundance of nodding timothy, purpled grapes and blushing clover for man and his silent servants, by fall will be buried the food of battle—bullets, bombs, shells. They call this thing an ammunition depot, a giant who will pounce on 18 square miles of the historic townships of Romulus and Varick, in the heart of Seneca County, strip them of their prosperous farms, historic churches and grange halls, and sow them with powder and shot.*[38]

As historian L. Dean Bruno observed, not only would there be the loss of the bountiful land, but also looming was the destruction of an entire community that had developed over generations.[39] More than 110 families were forced from their homes and farms in the Townships of Romulus and Varick. This strip of land, approximately eight miles long and four miles wide, had been worked by the same families for generations, many since the Sullivan Campaign of 1779. The thriving community, known as Kendaia, or Appletown, was located near the eastern shore of Seneca Lake in the Finger Lakes region of New York State. Farmhouses, barns, outbuildings, orchards and field crops were demanded from the citizens by the federal government.

Mr. and Mrs. John B. Lisk of Baptist Church Road, Kendaia. They had only three days' notice to quit their farm, where they had lived for thirty-five years. *Courtesy of* Syracuse Post-Standard.

My grandparents on both sides had farmed their land for more than thirty-five years. They were active in their community and looked forward to retiring among families and friends. Instead, in that summer of 1941, they had to find new farms and homes, move their livestock and harvest what crops they could before they were forced to leave. A few years ago, I was very surprised to find in an old trunk an article from the *Syracuse Post Standard*, July 26, 1941, with the headline, "Three-Day Notice to Quit Century Old Farm in Depot Area Fails to Dim Lisks' Patriotism."[40] These were my maternal grandparents, and all my life I had heard from my mother that the seizing of the farms and homes was a terrible and traumatic event. I had no idea that patriotism was a factor, but my grandmother, Edith (Googe) Lisk, was quoted in that article, "I'd rather give my farm to the government now to make America strong than to see another woman give her son's life to the defenses of the country when we didn't prepare."[41]

Despite the federal government's appeal for sacrifice and patriotism, not all of the citizens agreed with my grandmother. "There was no sense

This car was left in the road and locked, so the workmen picked it up and put it into the ditch in order to get the house by it. *Courtesy of the* Syracuse Post-Standard.

of patriotism; moving was just something we were forced to do by the government," said Aletha Hicks, age ninety-five, in an interview with Bruno.[42] During an interview later that summer in the *Geneva Daily Times*, Colonel M.E. McFadden, the Zone Constructing Quartermaster for New York, New Jersey and Delaware, emphasized that in determining the location of the depot, an "important point that we considered was the type of person living in this region, for with such an important depot in their midst it is vital that the Army's neighbors are 100 per cent Americans."[43]

This comment went beyond the typical themes of patriotism and sacrifice. It implied that instead of the creation of the Ordnance Depot being a burden, the people of Seneca County should be honored that the War Department considered them worthy of having their land taken in support of such a vital facility.[44] In the summer of 1941, Americans were divided over Roosevelt's preparations for war. Despite the federal government's appeal, the dispossession in Seneca County was opposed by some members of the upstate community. While the local county newspaper, the *Geneva Daily Times*, touted the government line, dailies from Syracuse, Elmira and Buffalo were more critical of the military's intrusion into local lands.[45]

On July 22, 1941, the first of the families were forced to move, my family among them. My grandparents, John and Edith Lisk, had to leave the farm they had worked for thirty-five years. Their home was more than one hundred years old; the farm was 157 acres. Grandfather Lisk was sixty-five years old and had always lived "a stone's throw" from his farm. My grandmother was sixty and had been born in Brooklyn. She first came to Romulus as a "Fresh Air Child" and returned in her twenties to marry my grandfather. During the Great Depression, she kept the family afloat with her thriving egg business, shipping her eggs to market in Brooklyn.

Their farm seized for the war machine, John and Edith started over at a new farm in Groton, about fifty miles away. They moved cows, chickens and other poultry. My grandfather was able to harvest fourteen acres of wheat and send it to Groton by truck; other crops, like oats and buckwheat, were left in the fields to be burned. They harvested during the day and moved their possessions, farm animals, equipment and crops at night, a long trip over bad roads. My mother recalled that the barns were pulled down on the third day regardless of what was in them. I can imagine the terrible confusion and effort all of this took with such little notice. Where you usually had the help of neighbors and relatives for such a move, every family was doing the same for themselves, so each must have been on its own. Florence Vargason, my grandmother's niece, says today, "We did what we had to do."[46] Like my Lisk grandparents, my grandparents on my father's side, LeRoy and Sadie (VanVleet) VanRiper had also lived and farmed in the seized area for thirty-five years. Grandfather LeRoy was a dedicated farmer; he bought a new farm with his son Albertus on Gilbert Road in Ovid. According to the local papers, forty-seven families bought farms elsewhere, thirty-five leased other farms and twenty quit farming altogether.

My parents, Barton and Emily (Lisk) VanRiper, were both schoolteachers, and they owned a house and small acreage on McDougall Road. The War Department confirmed the government's agreement to buy their three acres for $900 by letter and telegram, both dated July 23, stating that they had three weeks to vacate their property. However, another letter dated July 22 arrived the same day saying they had only

QM-RE Form, 38

Project Seneca Ordnance Depot, New York — Tract No. 64 A

Vendor Barton Van Riper — Contract No. 766 [illegible] 8078

WAR DEPARTMENT

Office Quartermaster General - Construction Division
Real Estate Branch

Notice of Acceptance of Option for Purchase of Land

Date July 23, 1941

Mr. Barton Van Riper
R. F. D. #1
Romulus, New York

Dear Sir:

Notice is hereby given that, on the 22nd day of July, 1941, the United States of America accepted the option dated the 19th day of July, 1941, for the acquisition of the tract of land situate in the County of Seneca, State of New York, more particularly described in the option.

A fully executed copy of the accepted option is inclosed.

For the Quartermaster General:

Very truly yours,

John J. O'Brien
JOHN J. O'BRIEN
Assistant

Incl.
Option

Left: Letter from the government of acceptance of the sale of property owned by Barton L. and Emily L. VanRiper. They expected, like others, to have three weeks to move. *Courtesy of Sally VanRiper Eller.*

Below: Telegram confirming the sale of property owned by Barton L. and Emily L. VanRiper. *Courtesy of Sally VanRiper Eller.*

THE COMPANY WILL APPRECIATE SUGGESTIONS FROM ITS PATRONS CONCERNING ITS SERVICE

1204

CLASS OF SERVICE

This is a full-rate Telegram or Cablegram unless its deferred character is indicated by a suitable sign above or preceding the address.

WESTERN UNION

R. B. WHITE, PRESIDENT — NEWCOMB CARLTON, CHAIRMAN OF THE BOARD — J. C. WILLEVER, FIRST VICE-PRESIDENT

SIGNS
DL = Day Letter
NM = Night Message
NL = Night Letter
LC = Deferred Cable
NLT = Cable Night Letter
Ship Radiogram

The filing time as shown in the date line on full-rate telegrams and day letters, and the time of receipt at destination as shown on all messages, is STANDARD TIME.

Received at

No 2 ck 24 2exa. Governors Island N.Y. 215AM 23.

Barton Van Riper,
RD I Romulus N.Y.

The united states of america accepted your option to sell three acres of land in seneca county on July twenty second nineteen forty one.

Somerville asst. to QM Gen
Washn D.C.

D 815AM

THE QUICKEST, SUREST AND SAFEST WAY TO SEND MONEY IS BY TELEGRAPH OR CABLE

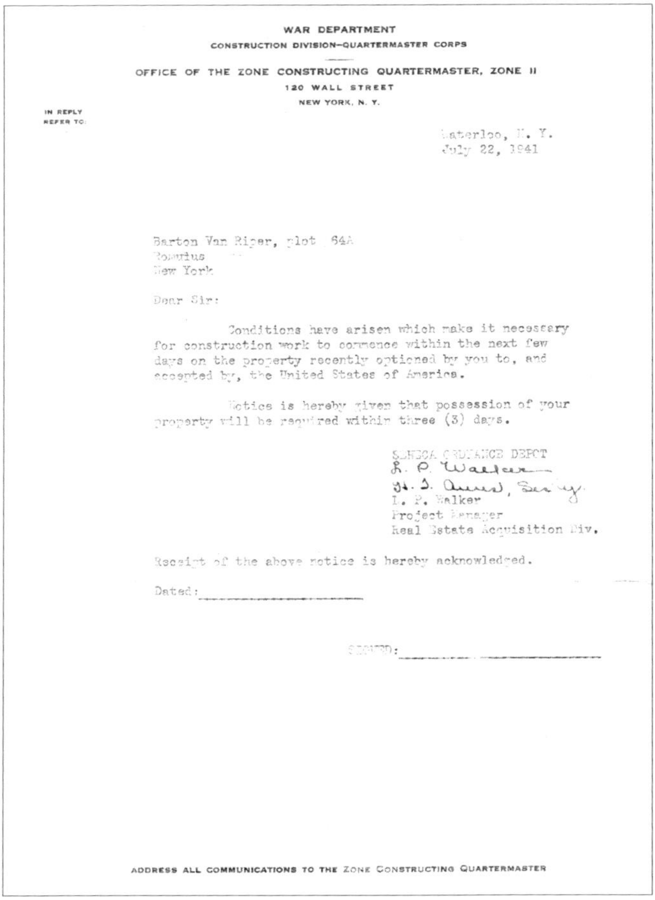

WAR DEPARTMENT
CONSTRUCTION DIVISION—QUARTERMASTER CORPS

OFFICE OF THE ZONE CONSTRUCTING QUARTERMASTER, ZONE II
120 WALL STREET
NEW YORK, N. Y.

IN REPLY REFER TO:

Waterloo, N. Y.
July 22, 1941

Barton Van Riper, plot 64A
Romulus
New York

Dear Sir:

Conditions have arisen which make it necessary for construction work to commence within the next few days on the property recently optioned by you to, and accepted by, the United States of America.

Notice is hereby given that possession of your property will be required within three (3) days.

SENECA ORDNANCE DEPOT
L. P. Walker
L. P. Walker
Project Manager
Real Estate Acquisition Div.

Receipt of the above notice is hereby acknowledged.

Dated: ____________

SIGNED: ____________

ADDRESS ALL COMMUNICATIONS TO THE ZONE CONSTRUCTING QUARTERMASTER

War Department letter to Barton and Emily VanRiper saying they had just three days to vacate their home, rather than the expected three weeks. *Courtesy of Sally VanRiper Eller.*

three days to move everything. Any buildings remaining after the third day were to be destroyed.[47] My father could buy back his poultry house for $75. He moved this "chicken coop" to Poplar Beach, Cayuga Lake, Town of Romulus, and built our home around it over the next several years. I was born in late October of that fall, and as in many families, I imagine there was concern about stress, hard work and worry during pregnancy.

The destruction of the barns and homes began. In an interview with Bruno on March 4, 2008, Kenneth Dean describes what happened to his family:

> *Kenneth Dean recounted that his father had just agreed to a sharecropping arrangement with a local farmer, and the Dean family was moving to their tenant farm when the base was announced. He was 11 years old*

> *at the time. The Dean family planned to raise corn, hay, wheat and beans on a 100 acre parcel of land. The Army allowed the Deans to gather their belongings. When they arrived at the farm, they found that government workers had shattered the front door and searched the house. Bulldozers were crisscrossing the fields, tearing up crops and outbuildings. Workers had even driven over and destroyed the family's horse-drawn hay rake. Days later, the house was flattened and the debris set on fire. Smoke drifted throughout the area. "There was no talk of patriotism or sacrifice," Mr. Dean stated, "just disbelief and disappointment. When the rumor first started to spread that the government might come in, few people thought it would ever happen."*[48]

Bruno's interview with Bob Sorenson, "Debating the Future of the Depot's Deer," *Ithaca Times*, May 2, 2007, provides further details of the government's techniques:

> *As a young boy, Bob Sorenson watched as the military removed his grandmother from her land. Decades after the traumatic events he recalled: "My grandmother had to leave her home, she wasn't too happy about it. There were cases where adult children had to come in and talk their parents out of their homes and off their land. Then the Army came in. They ran a steel cable through each house, fastened a steel train rail to one end of it, and hooked the other end to a bulldozer. They ripped the steel rail sideways through the house, which leveled it. Then they burned it. They wouldn't burn a standing house…There were a lot of unhappy people around here."*[49]

Houses were moved by permission from the government, at a cost of $300–$500 to move a house. Some were able to move their homes to nearby locations; the John T. White house was moved to a new location in Romulus with workmen finding it necessary to cut a tree limb that was blocking the progress down the road; others were able to salvage only parts of their homes. The *Geneva Times* reports, "At least three more houses will be moved within the next week; the former Peter Wyckoff home, purchased by the Misses Agnes and Anna M. McGrane; the Harry J. Williams house, purchased by Ward Newman, and the William O'Marra house to be moved to Romulus. All families were expected to be off the depot tract by the end of this week."[50] A Dean farmhouse was moved three miles to the village of Romulus, not far from the Romulus Central School. This house had been used by Army Colonel Paul Parker, who was in charge of construction of the Ordnance Depot, for his office since early July. He moved his office to a summer camp on Seneca Lake.[51] Mr. Charles Dunlap, an elderly farmer, was a great source for remembering who owned the land as many of the deeds were so old that Seneca County did not have a record of them. The government assigned an identification number to every house, barn and outbuilding in the seized area.

Several homes and barns were owned by members of the large McGrane family. One of the McGrane houses was moved to Main Street in Romulus rather than having it demolished; here it was used to house construction workers.[52] The Lucille Slike House was moved to Bush Pasture Road in Ovid. The J. Douglas Hinman home was moved to Romulus and situated on the southern side of Seneca Street in Romulus, where it is still a home.

Vineyards and grape farming were an important part of the local agriculture. Winfield A. Smith was the owner of a large vineyard and grape packing house that was later used as construction headquarters for the army. Other homes and farms taken and destroyed, except for some outbuildings used during construction, included the Marvin Brown home and the John McGrane home and barn. Houses rich in history such as the Erv Carroll home, where the first school in the region was held in the attic shortly after the Revolutionary War, were destroyed. Mr. Carroll was from England, and he remarked that he could never have had a home as nice as this in England.[53]

On March 4, 2008, Ed Montford talked with historian Bruno about just how painful this forced relinquishing of home and farm was.

> *Ed (and Emily)* [had] *recently married and were working the family farm in the summer of 1941. The land had been in his family's name since 1909. Mr. Montford described the farm as "120 acres of good tile-drained land, with nice buildings." The story told in the local newspapers was far different than what he and his wife experienced. "Government agents had no compassion and told me to accept the cut-rate offer of $7300 or they would simply condemn the land and take it. The farm was worth at least $15,000, but we ended up selling for*

Ed Montford moved from this home located one mile west of Romulus. The government developed a numbering and letting system for the parcels of property being taken for the depot. His wife, Emily, and his collie dog are also in the picture. *Courtesy of William Sebring.*

> *$7500." Like other families caught up in the wave of dispossession, Mr. Montford received conflicting messages from the government regarding the eviction date. The first letter he received granted him three weeks to gather his belongings and conclude affairs on the farm. But just days later, he found another letter in his mailbox—this time the government told him he had only three days to leave. Mr. Montford further recalled that they could not move all of their possessions within the 72 hour window, and when they tried to return to their farm for another load, a member of the military police blocked their path. "I gunned the engine and threatened to run him over—he finally stepped to the side." When they got to their home they found that their antiques, cherished by the family for generations, had been stolen. "Between the work of the looters and the men on the bulldozers, it was chaos," he said.*[54]

Moving must have been exciting and scary for the children. Alice (Updyke) Karlson remembers waiting anxiously in early August 1941 with her two sisters on their front porch, ready to be taken to their new home.

Norma Jean, Janet and Alice, daughters of Mr. and Mrs. George Updyke, on steps of their home on moving day. *Courtesy of the* Elmira Star-Gazette.

Alice still lives in Ovid, and she and members of her family attended the dedication of the New York State Dispossessed Family Marker on July 12, 2012, at Sampson State Park.

Of all the buildings destroyed by the federal government, perhaps the most important to the local residents were the churches. My family attended the First Wesleyan Methodist Church of Varick. The First Baptist Church of Romulus, established in 1795, was also known as the Kendaia Baptist Church. It was constructed during the ministry of Reverend John Caton, a veteran of the Revolutionary War and friend to General LaFayette. The last service here was September 7, 1941, Reverend B.A. Wagner, pastor. He and his wife moved to Phelps, New York, to retire. The church, which had lovely stained-glass windows, was sold for $17,000, was eventually dismantled and moved to Irelandville, New York, where it still stands, minus the stained-glass windows and the government identification number. The parish house was sold for $5,000.[55]

Young parishioners of the Kendaia Baptist Church urged all members to attend the last service, held on September 7, 1941. This church has the largest young people's group of any for many miles around, and the final service was attended by over one hundred people. A local paper, *The Rochester Democrat and Chronicle*, reported: "Patriotism combined with religious fervor made for an impressive final service conducted by the Rev. B.A. Wagner, pastor for the last 13 years."[56] Seneca Depot police patrolled the church grounds during this last service.[57]

Kendaia Baptist Church graveyard, oldest in the area, was also claimed by the War Department. Over the years, the military allowed local residents to maintain the cemetery under the watchful gaze of escorts. For only one day of the year, the Sunday of Memorial Day weekend, the military opened the Kendaia Cemetery to the public, and this continues to this day.

In this farming community, the National Grange, along with the churches, was a major social center for the communities. The Kendaia Grange Hall was taken and used by the government as the Office of Employment Services. This building is still standing—east of 96A on County Road 147. In an interview with Walter Gable in 2011, Phyllis Hudson said, "They [the depot] took a lot of the younger people. It affected the Grange. So many Grangers moved away. We kept some of the curtains. My son John has some of the materials. The Grange building was in tough shape."[58]

Until I found that 1941 newspaper clipping from the *Syracuse Post Standard* that first piqued my interest in what really happened in that traumatic year, I had never heard the word "patriotism" used in my family's accounts of this very difficult time in their lives. They only expressed sadness for their loss and resentment toward the government for being so heartless. Comments by L. Dean Bruno still raise questions for me—why did the farmers, schoolteachers and other residents of Romulus, Varick and Kendaia never protest their treatment? Maybe they did attempt some protests, but the local and statewide newspapers never reported any event of this nature. Were the newspapers just accepting what the government told them? Bruno's conclusion is that "compared to the potent forces of the federal government, local residents had little agency to act out or voice their displeasure."[59] Bruno goes on to say that "during the dispossession of the Kendaia farmers, not a single organized protest, demonstration or picket line was reported by the media. Given the government's campaign for sacrifice and patriotism, anyone who vociferously opposed the dispossession risked having their loyalties questioned. More importantly, the federal government held all the leverage in the 'bargaining' process. Local landowners either accepted the compensation offers of agents of the War Department, or had their lands condemned and taken. The federal government came to Seneca County because it could. Payment demanded compliance."[60]Or were there no protests to report because the citizens accepted their traumatic loss of home and land "as a sacrifice for the nation—a patriotic duty?"[61]

Was the rough handling of the landowners really necessary, or could the government have moved more deliberately in acquiring the Kendaia lands for the Ordnance Depot? Who were the looters of the homes and property that summer? If the government had guards posted to protect the farmers' homes and possessions during the three days they were given to move, why were so many cherished home furnishings taken?

These historical events occurred over seventy years ago, and until this summer of 2012, there had been no formal acknowledgement of the sacrifices of these people and their land. Thanks to the support of various donors, there is now a historical marker honoring the dispossessed families. It was placed near the entrance to the Sampson State Park and dedicated on July 12, 2012. My mother's cousin, Florence Vargason, ninety-three years old, and L. Dean Bruno were featured speakers. Eleven members of the dispossessed families were present for the ceremony. It was a bittersweet day for all.

CHAPTER 4
CONSTRUCTION IN 1941

Early in June 1941, the United States Government announced its intention to establish a munitions storage depot in central Seneca County near Romulus. The plans for the depot were conceived and executed with remarkable speed. The site was inspected on March 31 and April 1, and it was approved on June 11. Twelve days later, Colonel Paul B. Parker, Constructing Quartermaster, arrived in Kendaia and set up the government office. Within a few days, the work began.[62]

An office for coordinating the removal ("dispossession") of current property owners was established in the American Legion Home in Waterloo. Plans were made for the purchase of the necessary land and for the removal of those people living on this land. L.P. Walker of the Real Estate Division of the War Department was in charge. About one-fourth of the town of Romulus and one-fifth of the town of Varick was taken.[63]

William S. Lozier, Inc., of Rochester, was the architect-engineer for the Seneca Ordnance Depot. The New York City–based Poirier, McLane and John W. Harris Company was the general contractor.[64] Their previous contracts had included the Tri-Borough Bridge and Rockefeller Center. Bert J. Jones, the company's general superintendent, had supervised the building of sections of New York City's West Side Elevated Highway and the driving of thousands of uncased concrete piles—the first such piles ever driven in the city—for the Red Hook Housing Project. Ralph M. Burkhalter, the project manager, had worked several years on construction of the Holland Tunnel and, during World War I, had built concrete oil barges for the United States Navy.[65]

Colonel Paul B. Parker had graduated from West Point in 1916. He had gone to Mexico with General Pershing in the pursuit of Pancho Villa and then had served in France during World War I. He had retired and had been engaged in the construction business—with fifty-seven houses under construction in Arlington, Virginia—when he was recalled in February 1941 on twenty-four-hours' notice[66] and appointed inspector of construction for the U.S. Quartermaster Division of the War Department.[67] Two of his key assistants were Major Gerald P. Botsford[68] and First Lieutenant Harold C. Yelverton.[69]

The actual plan was to construct five hundred igloo-shaped magazines to house military supplies, each about ten feet high, eighty to one hundred feet in diameter, covered with earth, which would be seeded to grass. The initial completion date was May 1, 1942.[70] Electric service and lighting would have to be added, as would a commercial water system and sewer system. A permanent administration building as well as five hundred partially in-ground igloos and six above-ground magazines, fifty emergency foxhole shelters, a fire and guard house, a dispensary, four sets of living quarters, gate guardhouse, central heating plant, machine shop, twenty-three warehouses, an engine house and pumping plant and twenty platforms of railroad sidings for transfer of ammunition from igloos to care for shipment to seaboard ports would have to be constructed.[71] Also, there needed to be barracks to house the anticipated five hundred troops.[72] It was assumed that approximately three thousand temporary workers would be employed for this construction project. The initial estimated cost of the project was $8 million, with a weekly payroll of $250,000 to $300,000.[73]

It is important to state that this Seneca Ordnance Depot construction project was the largest construction project in the history of Seneca County up to that point in time.[74]

Initial Construction Work

Construction of the depot was started on July 9, 1941. Many preparatory activities had to be undertaken before formal construction of the munitions igloos could begin. The Kendaia railroad station had to be reopened and

Early on, much heavy construction equipment was brought in by rail and unloaded at the Kendaia station. *Courtesy of the Geneva Historical Society.*

made operational before heavy equipment could be brought in by train to undertake the major construction work. Another preparatory activity was to set up temporary headquarters. The old packing house of the Winfield A. Smith farms, about a mile from this hamlet of Kendaia, was used.[75] In these temporary headquarters, plank benches served for desks and nail kegs for chairs.[76] One newspaper characterized the scene as "bedlam," as staff members carried on their work at the temporary headquarters while office furniture was being moved in and partitions being built around it.[77] Another newspaper put it this way: "Officials are at work in every available corner. Chairs are at a premium and many a dignified official is surrounded, deep in conference with a group of technicians who are standing, hunched on the ground, or seated on overturned waste baskets and boxes. Offices are occupied while carpenters are driving the last nails. The sharp, vital odor of new lumber is borne down wind and everyone is working at top speed."[78] Until new electric power could be installed, it was not an uncommon sight for Colonel Parker and his associates to work by candlelight or making use of the newly acquired

Workers had to use kerosene lamps until electric lines were installed. *Courtesy of the Geneva Historical Society.*

hurricane lamps.[79] Additional telephone and electrical service had to be installed. Plans began as soon as possible to construct sewer lines and a sewage treatment facility, as well as a water system that would use Seneca Lake as a water source.

The initial target date for completion of construction was May 1, 1942. The project plans were to employ three thousand temporary workers with a total construction cost of $8 million. The completion date was moved up as events unfolded in 1941. By July 15, 1941, Colonel Parker was saying that the project was to be completed by April 1, 1942, with a total cost of $12 to $12.5 million.[80] Part of the reason for this was there were tentative plans for securing additional land for an airfield. This fact, coupled with the shortened timeline for completion of the project, led Colonel Parker to report publicly at that time that there would be two shifts of three thousand workers each. On August 1, 1941, Major Gerald P. Botsford announced that completion date for the project had been advanced to January 1, 1942.[81] By November 10, 1941, the target date for the completion of the five hundred igloos was advanced to December 1, 1941. Because of concerns about adverse wintry weather conditions, the engineers set November 15, 1941, as the target date.[82] The most important part of the construction project was the completion of the igloos, the last of which was completed on November 15, 1941.[83]

FORMAL DEDICATION OF THE FACILITY

The Seneca Ordnance Depot area was given the status of a military reservation with the U.S. flag formally raised at sunrise and lowered at sunset by uniformed guards. On August 21, 1941, the formal dedication took place, with impressive ceremonies. New York State Supreme Court Justice Lewis A. Gilbert of Lyons, New York, in his inaugural address stressed the significance of the Seneca Ordnance Depot as part of the government's defense program.[84] He said:

> *Here in rural Western New York in the heart of the Finger Lakes region, surrounded by farm lands where practically everyone is engaged in peaceful occupations, it is difficult for us to realize or appreciate the fact that a great part of the world today is in turmoil; that the peace and quiet of what we consider to be our normal daily existence is not the lot of civilized peoples generally, but that evil forces are abroad and at work today, which have, within the space of but a few months, uprooted and destroyed, perhaps forever, the peace and happiness of millions of people such as we, living in quiet countrysides, seeing only peace and happiness and wishing or doing harm to no one.*[85]

Following the colors-raising ceremony near the temporary administrative offices set up on the Smith Farm,[86] there was at the northern part of the depot a brief ceremony marking the pouring of concrete for the first igloo form. Mrs. Gilbert, wife of Supreme Court Justice Gilbert, broke a bottle of New York State champagne as a featured part of the program.[87]

Construction of the Igloos

By August 4, 1941, the new concrete plant began turning out concrete for igloos. Meanwhile the highway construction—some seventy miles of roads were needed for easy access to the igloos and to the barracks that would house some five hundred troops—was progressing at the rate of about two miles of roads a day.[88] Heavy trucks were entering the construction area at the rate of one a minute—some 960 trucks entering and driving over the narrow roads during the sixteen-hour working day.[89] Trucks were hauling in stone from the Hayts Corners quarry.[90] A third work shift was added in order to bring completion of the heavy work, including all igloos, by December 1, 1941.[91] The building of the igloos was stepped up from one a day to eleven completed a day.[92]

Between August 21 and November 13, 1941, some five hundred igloos were constructed to be used for munitions storage. These munitions igloos were designed by Leonard C. Urqhart, professor of structural engineering at Cornell University. Each was shaped like a tunnel on a

Workmen pouring concrete for the first munitions igloo. *Courtesy of the Geneva Historical Society.*

toy railroad. The concrete was about one foot thick at the top and two feet thick at the bottom. Entrance was gained through a door about three feet wide. Because of the scarcity of steel, the igloos were fitted with reinforced concrete doors that were cast onsite.[93]

An October 1941 article in the *Ovid Gazette* explained how an igloo was poured:

> *An igloo looks like a half of a huge oil drum cut the long way. It is 26 feet wide, 15 feet high and 60 feet long. At opposite ends are a door and ventilator. The steel frame is constructed of half hoops set about three feet apart. A huge metal reinforcement is welded together and swung into place by a crane. Metal plates are then fastened to the inside and outside ribs leave a space for concrete that will be 18 inches thick at the ground level and about eight inches on the roof.*
>
> *When an igloo is being poured, a mammoth crane stands on either side of the structure. From the end of the crane swings a cylindrical container with a hopper bottom that holds a cubic yard of cement. This is swung to a truck where a large mixer is in operation. A lever is pulled and the container filled. It swings back to the structure and the cement is dumped by a crew into square openings and rammed down with a mechanical vibrator. It takes about three hours for two cranes and two crews to pour one igloo. As fast as the cement hardens and is waterproofed, the igloos are covered with about two feet of dirt, landscaped and prepared for seeding to grass. They are staggered and placed about 400 or 500 feet apart.*[94]

A new national construction record was established at the depot when 13 igloos, as well as the floors for 16 more, were poured in one day—work involving the pouring of more than 3,100 cubic yards of concrete. By October 29, 1941, some 341 igloos, each about three hundred to four hundred feet apart, had been poured. Completed igloos were covered with earth.[95] On October 30, a record-breaking 16 igloos were concreted in a fourteen-hour period. The construction of the last block of 100 igloos was moving rapidly. Igloos in the final block were twenty feet longer than the 400 igloos in the four other sections of the depot. Another speed record was established when 159 cubic yards of concrete were poured in an hour.[96] By November 10, 1941, the floor of the last igloo was poured to the cheers of workmen, several of whom had helped pour the floor of the first igloo. This last igloo was completed November 15. The final pouring was photographed by a professional film crew that took night pictures of the event. "Under lights that made the igloo look like a Hollywood set, the pouring was put on film for future generations to have and to hold." The igloo was decorated with bunting as was the bucket used to pour cement. An American flag and a wooden "V" for "Victory" surrounded the magazine.[97]

The depot construction project was the largest single project being built by the Construction Division of the Quartermaster Corps in Zone II of the United States.[98]

One extensive newspaper article, based on the reporter's being a part of a group of newspapermen who were invited to see first-hand the construction project, gives good insight into the nature of the construction work:

> *On a vast 9680-acre Government reservation, 8600 workmen are racing grimly against time today, trying to finish the $11,000,000 Seneca Ordnance Depot before Winter sets in and halts heavy construction.*
>
> *Day and night they are building 500 igloos in which will be stored aerial bombs for the protection of the northeast coast of the United States against invasion by air or by sea. It's a nonstop, 24-hour a day, all-weather construction job, carried on with the speed required by emergency.*
>
> *Deep darkness had settled over this rural lake area Wednesday night, unbroken by the gleam of a star or beam of the moon as the clouds hung low, but construction went ahead uninterruptedly in the eerier glare of powerful floodlights.*
>
> *A group of newspapermen, Army officers and construction company engineers stood in the chilly, wind-swept area where workmen were pouring concrete on an igloo. It was a fascinating sight—giant cranes swinging huge buckets crazily in the air between half a dozen concrete mixers and the igloo.*
>
> *Each of these immense buckets carried 1.5 tons of concrete—and the job on that one igloo was only a small part of the whole picture. Here are a handful of figures to conjure with and visualize the immensity of this defense project:*
>
> *The tract of land on which the igloos are being built—(they're also known as storage magazines, and fox holes)—is two-thirds the size of*

Manhattan Island. Daily, 50,000 tons of dirt are moved; between one and two miles of road are built; 12,000 tons of stone are hauled in and 3000 yards of concrete are poured, enough to cover 1.5 miles of a two-lane state highway.

There are 92 generators in the field, and each generates 5 kilowatt hours—enough to illuminate a good-size town—turning night into day for the workmen who carry on in three shifts. Incidentally, there are 8614 construction men on the payroll-exclusive of a couple of thousand of office and clerical and similar workers. And tomorrow—payday—the construction payroll alone will be $420,000.

A. Bradford Squire, resident engineer for William S. Lozier Inc., Rochester, explained that several innovations have helped speed up the job, such as welding up mats of steel and having a crane lift them in place instead of the conventional method of putting up each rod individually.

"We save five hours' time building an igloo," he said. "We're trying to beat the weather. We want to get this exterior work done before snow falls. We started four months ago. Today concrete was poured on the 300th igloo. We will be substantially finished with all 500 igloos by Jan. 1."

"These men doing the work deserve a tribute—they're at it 24 hours a day and Sundays, too."

...When the igloo is completed it is covered with earth but not, as is generally supposed to camouflage it.

"You can't very well camouflage the igloos and besides it isn't as necessary as you might think," explained Maj. Gerald P. Botsford, executive officer. "The earth that will cover the igloos is to aid in maintaining as even a temperature as possible. Why don't you need camouflage? Well, in the first place, they stick up from the ground like sore thumbs. Secondly, they're not easy to hit. Don't forget that in an air raid a bomb must be released three miles from the target—that's due, of course, to the terrific speed at which the planes fly. Well, they can't aim at an igloo very well. The best an enemy airman could do would be to release his load between Seneca and Cayuga Lakes and hope for the best. And if he happened to make a lucky shot and score a hit on an igloo—well, we'd still have 499 left and could start rebuilding the destroyed one immediately."

Aerial bombs of all types will be stored in the igloos but how many, of course, depends on their dimensions. The bombs will be brought in

> *by train and placed in the igloos which are staggered—400 to 500 feet apart. And, by the way, the igloos are being built after today to the rhythm of music. A public address system was installed Wednesday with 39 speakers in various locations to give the men the soothing benefits of radio music as they go about their work. But it's grim music that could be given out by those bombs for which the igloos are being built."*[99]

Weather became a matter of serious continuing concern simply because freezing weather would damage the concrete essential to the building of these igloos. A weather bureau was established at the depot to forecast any changes that might affect the pouring of concrete. By short-wave radio, the Civil Aeronautics Authority supplied weather reports twice every hour from the control tower of the Syracuse airport. The weather information was sent out three times a day to the project's engineers and construction men so that imminent work schedules could be adjusted accordingly.[100]

Number of Workers Employed in the Construction Project

Initially, it was reported that there would be 3,000 temporary workers employed. By the end of July 1941, 400 workers and eighty pieces of heavy machinery were engaged in a "mile a day" road construction.[101] On August 1, 1941, there were 1,000 men employed.[102] By mid-August, 1,800 persons were employed at the depot project with a total of nearly 7,000 expected in four weeks.[103]

By August 25, 1941, there were 2,954 workers.[104] By early September, 3,100 were employed on the constructions phases.[105] By September 22, 1941, more than 5,700 were employed at the depot. By October 23, 1941, 8,614 construction men were employed on the project, exclusive of a few thousand office, clerical and similar administrative workers.[106] By October 27, 1941, there were 8,827 employed, with the payroll that week amounting to $424,234.29.[107] With the last igloo completed on November 15, 1941, the size of the labor force declined sharply. By November 19, 1941, construction forces were reduced by half. Approximately 1,000

Left: The Kendaia Grange Hall became the local employment office. *Courtesy of the Geneva Historical Society.*

Below: Men applied for jobs inside the Kendaia Grange Hall. *Courtesy of the Geneva Historical Society.*

Men came from great distances to get construction jobs at the depot. *Courtesy of the Geneva Historical Society.*

people were to be employed on winter construction. It was reported that construction was 80 percent complete by November 28, 1941, with 3,600 men still employed.[108]

Where These Workers Came From

By July 15, 1941, the New York State Employment Office in Geneva, New York, had set up a branch office at the Kendaia Grange Hall. People, mainly males for the construction work, went there to apply for jobs. Workmen that were hired had to be photographed and fingerprinted, pass a physical exam and take an oath of allegiance to the government of the United States.[109] The general contractors for the construction project made every effort to use local labor without causing a dislocation of workers in local businesses. Unemployed were to be the first to benefit, as well as young men on vacation from school or college.[110] The War Department appeared to be particularly proud of the new opportunities offered to young people by the defense program at Seneca Ordnance Depot and other depots. Unlike the dark years of the Depression, these defense programs were providing youths with opportunities to get specialized training in operating machines such as lathes, milling machines, shapers and drill presses, as well as training in blue-print reading, etc.—work skills for immediate jobs in building these depots but also skills that would enable them to later get good jobs in private industries.[111]

By early September 1941, when the work force totaled nearly 4,000, of which 3,100 were employed on the construction phases, about 50 percent of the workers were residents of Geneva, and 80 percent were from within a fifty-mile radius. Job applicants averaged one hundred per day.[112] At that time, the nature of the work being done by those employed was as follows: 25 percent carpenters, 35 to 40 percent laborers and the balance split up among iron workers, mechanics, masons, pipe fitters and so on.[113] By mid-July, Earl Finzar, business agent for the Geneva Federation of Labor, said all union carpenters who wanted to work were on the job.[114]

Colonel Parker stated on September 13 that the War Department had never sent out "a general call for labor." He added that, "We do not have control, however, over individuals who may come to this area on their own initiative." In terms of workers who could perform some very skilled work, he said, "In specific instances we have obtained skilled men needed to perform specific work when they were needed and when and only when the general contractors were prepared to hire them immediately."[115]

While as much as 80 percent of the workforce may have been "local" and the War Department did not issue any general call for labor, many men still flocked to the depot hoping to get hired. As early as July 15, there were reports that "long rows of autos with license plates indicating registration in Rochester, Auburn, Wolcott, Marion, Syracuse, Geneva, and other cities and towns in this part of the state were parked along the highway near the employment office."

Local residents reportedly were particularly upset with the "influx of Negro workers trying to get employment on the project. At the present time they are coming from as far away as Buffalo. They are sleeping in their cars now and are reported as having difficulty in finding rooms or other accommodations."[116]

Housing in Tents and Trailers and Health Problems

Housing was a concern on the part of Colonel Parker and his key staff from the very beginning of the project. Parker said, "It is hoped that Geneva and nearby communities will co-operate and absorb the personnel." Local residents made beds, if not full rooms, available in their homes for workers to rent. This went as far as instances in which lake cottages leased with a no sub-lease or rental clause were allowed by the landowners to make an exception for depot workers to stay in those cottages.[117] As the deadline for completion of the depot was moved up and more and more workers were needed, the housing shortage became more and more serious.

By late August 1941, it was nearly impossible to find lodging in Geneva, Ithaca or other smaller towns in the area. There were reports of some

This is an example of the makeshift housing that many workers and their family members lived in during the summer of 1941. *Courtesy of the Geneva Historical Society.*

A few families took their turn sleeping in an old bus instead of in their tents. Here, a county nurse is checking up on the health of the children. *Courtesy of the Geneva Historical Society.*

workers simply sleeping outdoors. Like many upstate newspapers, the *Syracuse Herald-Journal* on August 25, 1941, reported that the result of this housing shortage was "a growing number of tents and trailers in the vicinity of the depot. In fields near gas stations, where there is access to water and electricity, trailers and tent camps are springing up. Three and four children, with their parents, live in a single tent of seven feet square." One such family was the Manley Darrow family consisting of the two parents and three children. The Darrows, who were from Troy, New York, reported in that article that they had lived quite comfortably already for two weeks in their tent. They cooked their meals outdoors, picnic fashion. Mrs. Darrow said that the "entire family is clean and neat, but they were looking forward to a little better life when their new trailer was to be delivered on the following day." She added that she intended to send her two school-age daughters back to stay with her mother once the new school year began. The nearby Donald Peppard family, from Lancaster, Pennsylvania, was already living in a two-room trailer—one bedroom and a living room. They did their cooking over a miniature gas stove using bottled gas and electric lights secured by plugging in on the nearby pole. The Darrows and the Peppards, as well as other families living in tents and trailers near to gas stations, reported that "the bane of the tent wife's experience is the water situation. The entire supply had to be carried some distance."[118] A common sight was to have standing sacks of vegetables and fruits stored under the trailer and laundry hung from a clothesline between the trailer and a tree.[119]

These housing conditions raised serious health concerns. On August 24, the district health officer warned depot officials of the danger of bringing thousands of people into the area without observing proper health precautions. He was especially worried about the influx of workers and their families from other states. He urged vaccination against smallpox for each person and stressed the importance of clean water supplies and safe milk.[120]

The housing situation in the immediate Kendaia area was already serious. About five hundred people were living in tents and trailers, some homemade. Two families lived in chicken coops, some in sheds or autos and one in a barn. Three families, including children, lived in an old school bus, taking turns sleeping on the one cot available, or otherwise sleeping in their cars. About fifty tents and trailers were on land rented for two dollars a week with electricity. Robert Morley earned forty dollars each week working at the depot. His wife worked in a nearby restaurant. The Morley family had not looked for other living quarters as a result of his working hours and rumors of high rent costs. The Penner family erected a homemade trailer for sleeping and built a twelve-foot by six-foot shack, divided inside by canvas for cooking and eating purposes. When Mrs. Penner was asked if she would like to live in a house or room, she replied, "Why should I move? I have everything I want here."[121]

Soon, many farmhouses had trailers in their yards or fields, overtaxing private water and sewage facilities. By September 5, state health authorities declared wells were unsafe in 80 percent of the places furnishing accommodations for workers and trailers. Families were notified to buy milk in bottles—the only known safe milk.[122]

There seemed to be some misunderstanding as to who was to be blamed for the serious housing and health problem. Colonel Parker on September 11 declared that the "trailer camp problem, at the present time, is solely a matter of enforcement of health laws." He described as "mis-informed and ill-advised" recent press reports that the "workers are being forced to live in trailers." He went on to say:

> *As a matter of public information, it should be stated now and here that, the housing problem and other social problems incident to a project of this kind were approached with care and forethought* [sic] *before construction work was undertaken here. Through the office of the Constructing Quartermaster for this project, the local communities affected were informed of the nature of the project and asked to make a survey of their housing facilities. All of these communities quickly responded and the sum total of their surveys indicated that housing would be sufficient.*
>
> *At the same time a private check was made which indicated that facilities would be adequate. Not a single community up to the present time has reported to this office that its housing facilities are actually over-taxed. It would seem, therefore, in all fairness that these communities ought to be the first to discover any lack of housing facilities.*
>
> *When this project was being started and when the local communities were being consulted, it was pointed out by this office, not once but many times, that trailer camps would not be favored and it was suggested that they should be tolerated only when housing facilities were actually exhausted…*
>
> *What has actually happened in the vicinity of Kendaia is this: A number of nomadic workers, some of them inured to a migratory life, have set up trailer camps under conditions which would not be tolerated for a moment on this military reservation. All workers on this project are receiving good wages and many of them are getting better wages than they have received in years. There is no question here of these persons being unable to pay for housing. These workers are simply choosing the line of least resistance and camping on property over which the QMC, Construction Division has no authority whatsoever.*

Colonel Parker went on to point out that in similar cases in other communities deriving similar economic boom from such temporary defense construction projects, the local residents and officials have realized the value of "making some local investment in decent living conditions for the trailer-dwellers that they harbored."[123]

This was the only safe well for all the workers and their families living in Kendaia in temporary housing. *Courtesy of the Geneva Historical Society.*

Two cases of typhoid were reported in Lodi. The two victims—both children—lived in a home that took in depot workers as boarders and roomers. These two were taken as patients to the Auburn City Hospital. An average of ten cases of diarrhea occurred daily in Kendaia. Local physicians were "watching" four of those cases as they suspected that one might well be typhoid and the other three dysentery. Two cases of tuberculosis were found, "among the transients just south of Kendaia." Both cases were so advanced that they had to be moved from the area in ambulances. One was taken to the Onondaga Sanatorium and the other, too ill to be moved so far, was taken to the Hermann Biggs Memorial Hospital at Ithaca. Another typhoid suspect was brought to the Geneva General Hospital to be kept under observation.[124]

The only well safe for drinking water for these new "residents" in Kendaia was the well near the schoolhouse.[125] "In a county noted for sparkling lakes, no safe water was available except for an insufficient amount trucked in from Geneva." Although a number of new toilets were brought in to the Kendaia area, the health officials described conditions as like a "hobo jungle." Public health nurses were used to show women how to treat the water. Two clinics were established to provide free inoculation against typhoid fever and smallpox. Children were given dental care and diphtheria anti-toxin.[126]

It needs to be pointed out the lack of pure drinking water and other health and housing problems at the Seneca Ordnance Depot

Without a public sewer system, workers and their families had been using outhouse facilities like this. *Courtesy of the Geneva Historical Society.*

construction project were unique, since similar problems had not arisen in other defense projects in this state. It appears that it became such a problem for this project basically because the stepping up of the timeline for completion of the depot project led to a rapid population growth with the influx of so many workers.[127]

On Saturday, September 13, 1941, Congressman John Taber held an informal conference with town, county and ordnance officials in the schoolhouse at Romulus to discuss all angles of the situation. To help alleviate concerns about water problems in the hamlet of Romulus, Congressman Taber said that he would do all he could to get the hamlet connected to the ordnance depot's water system. He felt the cost could be funded through the federal Lammam Act, which provided federal financing for projects made necessary through construction of military bases, depots and barracks.[128]

Newspapers reported on September 13 that the following Monday and Tuesday (September 15 and 16, 1941), a conference of state and federal housing officials, state and district health officers and ordnance depot heads would take place to deal with the housing and health problems arising from the depot construction project. Sixty-five families were living in the camp area at Kendaia. Some 540 were living in tents, nearly all without wooden floors; 13 were living in trailers; 2 were living in chicken coops; 1 in a barn; and others were living and sleeping in automobiles. The nearby hamlet of Romulus had several problems, chief among which was the lack of a water system. Village water came chiefly from wells, although the school had its own water supply and its own sewerage system. The coming of fall and cold weather brought the housing and health problems of depot workers to a focus. The articles went on to report that health officials did not object to workers and their families living in properly fitted tents and house trailers, but that they were very much concerned over the lack of drinking water and sewage systems. In one group of tents, a serious situation had been created because the campers had not bothered to dig latrines, pits for garbage or for dish water. Instead, they simply used the woods in the rear of the tents for toilet purposes and grounds surrounding the area were in "bad condition." Clothes had been washed in water from polluted wells in spite of the best efforts of the health officers and the nurses, and covers had been pried off wells plainly placarded with warning signs. All wells except one were polluted and were being doused with lime. Dr. Griswold also pointed out that the State Health Department has nothing to do with housing. "It cannot compel the people to live in approved homes. Its function is to prevent disease outbreaks and advise and aid in health matters." This work was being done.[129]

The two-day conference of state and federal housing officials, state and federal health officers and ordnance depot heads resulted in a five-point plan to end the health menace at Kendaia:

1. There would be the establishment of a homes registration office in Waterloo under the auspices of the Division of Home Defense Coordination so that incoming workers would obtain up-to-the-minute information on available living quarters.
2. A trailer camp would be established at the Waterloo fair grounds, under the supervision of the Federal Farms Securities Administration.

3. There would be an organized effort on the part of union officials to require new workers to avail themselves of the facilities provided by the housing registration office so that new workers, in so far as they are able, would provide themselves with suitable quarters before they could go to work.
4. Workers who fail to comply with state health requirements for no good reason would be dismissed from their employment at the depot.
5. There would be proper use of all existing agencies to the end that individuals would not suffer as a result of this joint effort to end the Kendaia health menace.[130]

To help implement that first point in the plan, in advance of the conference itself, New York lieutenant governor Charles Poletti sent a score of state troopers in on Saturday, September 13, 1941. These state troopers, under Lieutenant John P. Roman of the Oneida barracks, made a house-to-house canvass of "Seneca County from one end to the other and even covered sections of Ontario County."[131] The survey was begun that Saturday morning and completed by 2:00 p.m. on Monday. The Ontario County communities canvassed were Clifton Springs, Phelps, Seneca Castle and Oaks Corners.[132] This resulted in a list of as many as 1,500 rooms and a number of houses that could be rented by the additional depot workers needed in the next month. Former Seneca County Clerk Charles C. Inshaw was appointed by the federal government's Division of Home Defense Coordination to open a listing and allocation office in the court house at Waterloo. Newspapers were asked to make another appeal that any householder who had an unused room to notify Mr. Inshaw.[133]

On Saturday, September 20, 1941, Lieutenant Governor Charles Poletti was taken on a tour of inspection of the depot project. His summary comment was that the "Army is doing a bully job." While at the depot, it was also disclosed that the defense investigating committee of the U.S. Senate would be visiting the Seneca depot to "study the Kendaia situation, where a strike and complaints of poor housing have hampered construction."[134]

Getting back to the specifics regarding the plan of action growing out of the two-day conference, the Waterloo Fairgrounds site was chosen over other areas under consideration. Those other sites included the abandoned Ovid high school building, the mill buildings in Waterloo and the abandoned CCC buildings at Cayuga Lake State Park.[135] The fairgrounds site was chosen primarily because it had a plentiful supply of water and a suitable sanitary sewer system. Arrangements were made with the Seneca County Agricultural Society to rent the inland area of the racetrack for two years for $850. The project was known as Waterloo Trailer Park, Defense Project No. 18.

On October 2, 1941, it was announced that President Roosevelt had approved construction of the trailer camp, displacing the Waterloo High School football team that had used the fairgrounds as its home field. Some $46,000 was allocated to extend water mains throughout the fairgrounds and to install adequate lighting. Each government-owned trailer could accommodate a family of four and rented for $6.50 a week. Imported from Erie, Pennsylvania, each trailer had a gasoline cooking and kerosene heating stove, refrigerator, water tank, sink, cupboards and bed. The trailers were set up on each side of two streets created inside the half-mile racetrack. Each trailer was jacked up and secured to the ground. Trailers were spaced twenty-five feet apart. Laundry and bathing facilities were provided under the grandstand. Floral Hall was improved to serve as headquarters for a staff of ten. Workers providing their own trailer could rent a space; the weekly rental rate was about $3.50.[136]

On October 4, 1941, all trailer occupants were ordered to evacuate the land around the depot, where conditions were described by Charles Agar, the state senior sanitary engineer, as "beyond belief." According to a survey that had recently been completed by Mr. Agar and George Moore, the district sanitary engineer, there were 64 trailers in camps at Kendaia; 17 families in temporary houses (shacks, chicken coops and automobiles); 139 trailers in other camps in the county; 1,761 people living near the depot; 512 people in temporary houses; 118 families in temporary houses; 127 children in temporary houses; and 762 people using contaminated water. His report further showed that there were 112 hotel and boardinghouse rooms, 90 rooming house rooms and 46 trailer camps total in Seneca, Tompkins, Ontario and Schuyler Counties.[137]

Only families were accommodated at the Waterloo camp. (Single men working at the depot were expected to secure housing at the Home Registration Office.) The federal government brought in fifty trailers, and there was space for one hundred privately owned trailers. First priority was to be given to those who had been living in tents, barns and chicken coops and other temporary structures and then to those who had been living in trailers.[138]

By October 7, 1941, some 50 families were living at the "Waterloo Trailer Town," as it became known locally. Nearly all government trailers were occupied by October 11, and twenty-nine more government trailers were ordered. The population of the trailer city reached about four hundred by October 14—a total of 111 families. Two youngsters, ages ten and eleven, were assigned as "junior police officers" to aid the eighty-five youngsters in the government trailer camp as they came to and from school or moved about the trailer park.

The federal government provided trailers for families of depot construction workers. *Courtesy of the* Rochester Democrat and Chronicle.

To help alleviate the unsanitary conditions that had existed in many camping grounds, rigid new health inspections were instituted. *Courtesy of the Geneva Historical Society.*

It needs to be added that there were seven other trailer camps, near Kendaia, that were operating now with permits. All had safe drinking water, adequate toilet facilities and pasteurized milk delivered in bottles. Not all of the families had wanted to be forced to move to a "permitted" trailer camp or to the Waterloo Trailer Park. They stated that they considered it "far more healthful from their standpoint to live in private areas in open country than to be forced to reside in the public trailer camp." One woman characterized the State Health Department's order as "an interference with the inherent rights of the people."[139]

The trailer camp was dedicated on Sunday, November 3, 1941.[140] Members of the Warner Van Riper Post American Legion provided a color guard and bugler for the raising of the American flag on a new pole erected in front of Floral Hall. Major Botsford praised those who assisted in the establishment of the camp, which was "keeping our workers healthy and happy" as well as preventing any epidemic. He added that there had not been a single fatality on the depot project. The chief of the Resettlement Division stated this trailer camp was the first of its kind in the nation for any depot project. It was also the first camp in the country to have a health clinic.[141]

At the close of 1942, the *Seneca Falls Reveille* reported that the Waterloo Trailer Camp had a greater population per square mile than any other place in the county. (This trailer park was still in use because of the construction at the Sampson Naval Station, as well as people who were working at the Seneca Ordnance Depot after construction was completed.) Two hundred families (more than seven hundred people) were living in the area inside the fairgrounds racetrack. Wooden sidewalks led from the street to each trailer door. All government-supplied trailers were painted olive drab. There were two types of trailers—expandable and non-expandable. The expandable trailers were constructed so that the sides could be pulled out so as to provide approximately 25 percent more room inside the trailer. These expandable trailers rented for $7.50 per week. Electric power lines ran to each trailer home, but water was only piped to several places in the area, not to each home. Showers and toilet facilities were provided at a number of places in the trailer village in pre-fabricated buildings that could be dismantled and used at another project at some future date. Recreation facilities were limited, but there was space in the administration building for bingo and dances. There was no planned recreation for the children, but they had the whole fairgrounds for play. A State Public Health Nurse was on duty every day, providing dental, preschool and prenatal clinics.[142]

Residents of the trailer village came from eleven states: Maine, Pennsylvania, New York, Rhode Island, Indiana, New Jersey, Tennessee, Texas, Kentucky, Florida and Connecticut. The largest number came from the New York City metropolitan area.[143]

Worker Strikes During Construction

On August 22, 1941, more than two hundred of the workers quit work, even though they were not legally able to strike against the government. They complained of illness resulting from contaminated water. They sought a $0.25-per-hour raise from their $1.50 per-hour rate. After discussion with Colonel Parker, who told them that their wages were fixed in Washington, D.C., they returned to work.[144]

Then in mid-September, operating engineers went on strike and were joined in sympathy by the men employed as oilers. The engineers were being paid $1.50 per hour and demanded an increase of $0.25 per hour. In a meeting with representatives of the contractors, Poirier, McLane and John W. Harris Company, a deal was worked out to end the strike. The Department of Labor agreed to raise the hourly rate to $1.62½, which the labor union accepted.[145]

On September 18, 1941, when Major Botsford spoke to the annual convention of the New York State Town Highway Superintendents, he told of "organized attempts to create labor unrest among 3,000 workers at the $8,000,000 project." He said the move was similar to those in other defense projects in the nation. He said that there were stories circulating among the workers that included tales of army officers "driving the men to death, of bodies being dumped into concrete mixers, and of thousands of Negroes being recruited in the South to take away the jobs of local men."[146]

On October 1, 1941, truck drivers hauling stone from the quarry near Hayts Corners halted operations for several hours, seeking their alleged promised pay increase. The truck drivers were reassured they would get the expected raises, and they returned to work. It was reported that even this one to four hours of work stoppage (there were varying reports of the actual length of the work stoppage) slowed the construction work for the day. This came at a time when the construction time schedule had been stepped up from one to eleven igloos daily.[147]

Kendaia and Romulus Hamlets Become "Boom Towns"

Prior to the construction of the depot, both hamlets of Kendaia and Romulus could probably have been characterized as "just another small town, unknown to most people living outside a twenty-five mile radius."[148] One newspaper described Kendaia as a "drowsing country crossroads with a lonely railroad station closed for lack of business until a few days ago." It went on to say, "Kendaia has suddenly come to life as workmen, cranes, power shovels and other machinery clear a wide area near the railroad station for construction machine shops and storage yards."[149] By late summer, Kendaia had swelled to a population of over six thousand. This should not be that surprising, given that Kendaia was the closest "community" to the construction base because it had a station on the Lehigh Valley Railroad.

In mid-July, the New York State Employment Office opened a branch office in the Kendaia Grange No. 64 Hall. As a result, long rows of automobiles from many upstate New York communities were parked along the highway near this office. Just south of Kendaia, the former warehouse of the Smith Farm was the "temporary" headquarters for the construction project.[150] By mid-August, a newspaper reported that you "can't find a place to park your car in…[this] village of 300…A cross-roads school has become a first-aid station. There are hot-dog stands in hastily-erected tents. Trailer camps clutter up the nearby fields."[151]

C.A. Crane was the proprietor of the General Store at Kendaia. He reported in early September 1941 that his business had increased 400 percent with the establishment of the depot on the reservation across the road from his property. "Where once stood kegs of salt mackerel, dill pickles, nails, crackers and tins of kerosene, there are now piled up cases of empty pop bottles."

The sale of soft drinks had increased because of the difficulties in obtaining sanitary drinking water. Mr. Crane estimated that he was selling about ten cases of soft drinks daily—240 bottles. Each Wednesday he unloaded a truckload of soft drinks at a cost of seventy-five dollars. Often that was not enough of a supply to last him until the next Wednesday. Mr. Crane replaced the old yard goods counter with an ice cream chest. Other items sold in great quantities were smoked meats, tobacco and baked goods. Foods sold were of a variety that could be quickly prepared for serving, as hundreds in the vicinity were living in tents or trailers. Store hours were 8:00 a.m. to 8:00 p.m., but customers would come in at any hour if the doors were open. Mr. Crane and his wife and three children worked to keep up with demand. In the side yard to the store were ten trailers. Their owners had begged to be allowed to "stop" there. The gas pumps were often empty because his store's gas allowance (in light of wartime rationing) was based on his sales in July when five hundred people were working on the depot project—not the current work force of over three thousand. The Cranes had no time to make plans for spending their suddenly increased income. He admitted, however, that "we get pretty tired."[152] Mr. Crane probably thought that this "Depot construction project" crush of business would subside once the depot construction was completed. The decision to build the Sampson Naval Station nearby in 1942 meant that there would be lots of sailors-in-training as customers throughout the duration of World War II.

The situation in Romulus was quite similar. Businessmen in Romulus reported an increase of sales from 150 to 200 percent. The local population was estimated to have more than doubled. The typical small town shops became so taxed that many stores had to employ additional help. This was true for local barber and local gas station owner Roy Coryell. He got his wife to help him out during rush hours until the 7:00 p.m. curfew. The local post office, headed by Postmaster George McGrane, was handling double the amount of business from the previous year. He noted that receipts skyrocketed because many depot workers used money orders to send money back home for their families. To keep up the volume of mail, the postmaster had to burn plenty of "midnight oil," besides relying on his assistants and rural delivery men as well as three former postmasters who came back to work temporarily. Within the hamlet, private homes provided rooms for one hundred roomers. The Romulus Hotel added at least fifteen additional beds for depot workers and fed many boarders who slept in tents, trailers and private homes nearby. An abandoned store at the corner of Main and Cayuga Streets was reopened as a delicatessen/restaurant, staying open twenty-four hours a day to help feed the hungry depot workers, truck drivers and guards who changed shifts every eight hours. The vacant rooms over the Parks funeral establishment were quickly furnished with twelve beds for workers. Traffic was heavy day and night on the roads with the workers going to and from work as well as the many trucks in and out of the depot construction site. One newspaper described the situation as "like moving New York's Times Square into the village of Romulus." Speed limits were set up through the hamlet, especially near the Romulus Central School.[153]

Nearby Geneva also experienced a business boom. Retail trade business increased as much as 30 percent over the previous year. So many people were now employed that relief rolls had dropped practically to levels before the Depression. Some one thousand Genevans were employed at the depot project.[154] Three thousand depot project workers were living in Geneva. Hotels, restaurants and diners were doing a "landoffice business." Some businesses, however, that were not engaged in the production of war materials worried that their businesses would suffer when their surplus stocks of metals and other materials affected by "war priority" were used up. Similarly, retailers found that the prices for all of their merchandise were rising rapidly, causing them not to make the great profits they hoped. Another problem was that they found it hard to hire additional workers because the depot construction project paid higher hourly wages than they felt they could afford to pay.[155]

Some Interesting Construction Facts and Information

There were two shifts of work crews. The first shift was 6:00 a.m. to 2:30 p.m., with half hour for lunch. The second shift was 2:30 p.m. to 11:00 p.m., with half hour for a meal. The second shift worked under floodlights after darkness fell, with mobile generators used.[156] By mid-August, 1941, a third work shift was added to complete work before "winter sets in."[157]

While the work was pressure-packed, at least one humorous story came out of all of this. Despite all the construction noise at the headquarters, a nesting guinea hen was setting on thirty-two eggs alongside the warehouse. Lumber was to be piled right on the spot where she was nesting. Workmen built a barricade so trucks could not back into the nesting guinea hen. The next day fluffy guinea chicks began to hatch.[158]

The local housing shortage for depot construction workers became such a serious problem that Seneca County Sheriff Herbert H. Yells at one point provided temporary housing in the Seneca County Jail for ten employees at the Seneca Ordnance Depot at Kendaia who couldn't find accommodations elsewhere in the county. Sheriff Yells reported that he put up a number of beds in the basement dining room of the jail to house the depot workers until they could find rooms.[159]

Four Jordan brothers were involved in the construction project. Frank J. Jordan was the vice-president of the general contracting firm of Poirier, McLane and J.W. Harris Company. Bert J. Jordan was the general superintendent of the depot project. Vincent Jordan and James Jordan were assistant superintendents. All except James worked full-time at the depot site itself during construction.[160]

Some statistics announced by construction executives were reported in a November 13, 1941 newspaper article. It was an $11 million project in terms of cost. Some 8,800 workers had been employed in the construction. The job had involved 917,358 square feet of magazine area, about twenty miles of railroad and more than seventy miles of roads. The construction program included seven miles of water lines and thirty-six miles of drainage pipes. For the construction of the igloos,

The four Jordan brothers were all directly involved in the construction of the depot in *1941*. *Courtesy of the* Syracuse Post-Standard.

some 302,200 square yards of land had been cleared; 67,020 cubic yards of soil excavated; 120,643 cubic yards of concrete poured; 2,600 tons of steel rods used; 1,100 tons of steel mesh. On October 18, 1941, the most igloos—eighteen—were poured on a single day. Seventy-eight igloos were poured during the week ending October 22.

There had been some delay in the federal government supplying its trailers to the Waterloo fairgrounds camp. When Mrs. Eleanor Roosevelt learned about this on November 1 while in New York City, she "deftly cut through national defense red tape by personally telephoning the White House." She stepped into a telephone booth at the Hotel Pennsylvania and talked directly to her husband, the president, for just one minute. She then returned to a federal advisory council meeting to report that "the matter would have her husband's immediate attention."[161] When she was asked how long it took her to get the president to act, she replied, "About one minute. I never use up any more time than I have to."[162]

As the depot construction work was winding down in November 1941, a chief topic of conversation among many of the temporary depot workers from outside of the immediate area was where these workers were going after this project was completed. "The two leading places were Kentucky and Texas, with many of the employees planning to spend the winter basking in the sun of Florida. Wherever they go they expect to be on their way early next year, if not sooner."[163]

An article in the *Geneva Daily Times* said, "To the casual visitor and to the employee alike the most striking thing about the depot is the fact that it is in the advanced stage that it is in. One is struck daily by the wonder of modern architecture and construction which has enabled this project to be completed so far ahead of schedule. It may well be said to be a monument to this nation's determination to resist aggression. The catchword has been 'Time Is Short' and the men on the job have never lost sight of it."[164]

Additional Construction

By the end of 1941, six aboveground magazines were completed.[165] Work was continuing on the permanent administration building and various utility structures.

This 1942 aerial view shows some of the concrete block warehouses constructed that year. *Courtesy of the Romulus Historical Society.*

This is part of the sewage treatment facility that had to be constructed. Except for the two main railroads lines, the property acquired for the depot was seriously lacking in necessary infrastructure. *Courtesy of the Geneva Historical Society.*

In August 1942, a concrete batch plant was opened just south of the Romulus Central School building. It provided the concrete blocks that were used to build several warehouses south of the main gate on Route 96. Some housing quarters were completed in 1943.[166] With this construction work completed, the depot began its primary mission of receipt, storage, maintenance and supply of ammunition.[167]

CHAPTER 5
DURING WORLD WAR II

Following the Pearl Harbor attack and the formal entry of the United States into World War II, the situation at the Seneca Ordnance Depot took on an even greater urgency. The spring 1942 decision to construct the Sampson Naval Station added still more traffic congestion to the mid-county area. Given that clogged highways preventing the swift movement of French troops to the front had contributed to the fall of France, the state police and the army developed alternate routes for emergency use, as well as plans for clearing the highways for possible troop movements.[168]

In the foreword to a brochure of information distributed to depot workers, Depot Commanding Officer Colonel Arthur E. Elliott had the following to say about the role of the depot workers during World War II:

> *What is the Seneca Ordnance Depot? On the map it is twenty square miles of land situated between Seneca and Cayuga Lakes.*
>
> *What makes it tick? People—hundreds of people like you and those around you.*
>
> *Be ever mindful that you are an important part of the very essential industry supplying our combat forces with the ammunition and supplies they need. Your interest and effort to get shipments out on schedule is definite assurance that you realize how essential the success of the depot operations rest with you.*

In order to regulate this flow of ammunition and supplies, one of your most important jobs is to receive and store it properly so that there will always be on hand what may be needed and ready for shipment…

…This is our Depot, this is our country and we must and will join this war to keep the freedom that makes this all ours. We are a part, a great part of this war. We are the working part and only with work will we stay a part.

You are taxpayers paying the price of this war and what you do each day you are doing for yourselves…[169]

A July 23, 1943 newspaper article reported Colonel Elliott's public disclosure of the role that the Seneca Ordnance Depot was to play in the mission of Army Ordnance Field Service:

Under the newly received instructions Seneca operates as an export advance storage depot for boxed parts and supplies for automatic weapons, small arms, artillery, fire control instruments, tanks and vehicles, including combat vehicles.

As a reserve depot, Seneca stores such major items as automatic weapons, small arms, artillery, fire control instruments, tanks and vehicles, including combat vehicles, plus their spare parts, supplies, tools and equipment. The depot is responsible for retail distribution of automatic weapons and their organizational spare parts, tools and accessories within a prescribed area.

In its ammunition department, Seneca acts as a back-up depot for the receipt, storage, surveillance and distribution of all classes of ammunition and explosives except chemical ammunition, for normal distribution through east coast ports of embarkation. As an area depot, Seneca stores for issue to using military organizations various types and qualities of small arms ammunition for training and other purposes.

Seneca also operates a "popping plant," which is an establishment for burning out remaining particles of explosives in fired small arms and artillery cartridge cases as a step toward their renovation and re-use.

Subsidiary, but nevertheless important, functions include preservative maintenance of Ordnance material in storage, and maintenance and repair, so far as shop facilities permit, of all automotive and materials handling equipment used at the depot.[170]

According to a 1943 Syracuse newspaper, wartime changed the employees and the atmosphere of the depot:

> *Where once the Senecas shaped their flint-tipped arrows for battle, today sprawls vast Seneca Ordnance Depot charged with the mission of storing all classes of ordnance supplies and ammunition for reissue to troops in continental United States and for shipment overseas….*
>
> *More than 3000 workers, a high percentage of them girls, mothers, and even grandmothers, come daily to labor in the 20-odd vast warehouses where the munitions, arriving from factories, are assembled into complete units and prepared for shipment to the front lines. Not alone for plowshare, but here the skillet, has been beaten into a sword, for the numbers of women doing carpenter work, lifting and hauling heavy material and carrying out other normally male jobs, are increasing daily as men are drained off by the armed services.*
>
> *More than 600 women Ordnance workers, known as "Wows," wheeling large trucks over the area's miles of roadways and operate fork-lift cranes, trundling heavy bombs, machinery and vehicles from waiting boxcars to storage upon their arrival from domestic sources and the reverse of this process when assembled units are shipped out of the depot. We saw one young mother thrust the prongs of her fork-lift crane under the belly of a one-ton demolition bomb in a boxcar, wheel it across a loading platform and roll it into a waiting truck—all with the lack of concern with which she might poach an egg.*
>
> *There was a distinct sense of treading on the crater floor of a sleeping volcano as we entered the miles long, highly restricted area where millions of pounds of explosives are stored in concrete-domed, underground shelters, called "igloos." Ventilators in the massive igloo metal doors are set to slam shut automatically by devices similar to sprinkler systems, should brush fires sweep near the powder magazines. Their elliptical domes are strong enough to withstand shock of a light bomb…*
>
> *We touched and saw in heartening amounts large projectiles destined to be fired from America's newest mobile tank, destroyers used by the British Army when it put the Afrika Korps into headlong flight from Egypt. Biggest bombs handled, to date, at the Seneca Depot were 4000 pounders, shipped up from Delaware in December with "Merry Christmas you can have them," painted on their exteriors. It is expected*

soon that more of these and some, perhaps, double their size will be clearing through S.O.D. The extreme care and intricate operations required simply to take them from boxcars and store them opens a glimpse of the tremendous job it must be to put 1000 planes over Germany in a one-night bomb-raid. Although one of these raids would empty several igloos, bomb production might cease tomorrow and Seneca Ordnance Depot could keep on shipping its daily capacity for almost six months....

Final stop in the tour of the igloo areas was a visit to one shelter where shot and shell was arrayed in ascending order of its fire power, from the well-known .22 to the biggest on hand. There were clips of cartridges for the Garand rifle, machine gun web belts ready for firing, armor piercing shells, parachute flares, cluster bombs for anti-personnel use, bomb fins and timers. We were shown aerial depth bombs for Navy use and several restricted items about which no more can be written than the fact that they present visual proof America is keeping pace with the changing demands of modern warfare.

Upon leaving the igloo area all pocket matches and cigarette lighters, surrendered by the newsmen as they entered, were returned except some large kitchen-type matches which had been summarily destroyed.

Workers here can make only one mistake, an officer remarked as the tour stopped at a warehouse where girls and women were dipping hand grenades, painted yellow to denote "high explosive," in vats of olive drab paint.

Reason for the change over from yellow to muddy green stems from battle-line experience, we were told, during which it was realized bright colored stores and ammunition, abandoned in case of a withdrawal, were more easily discovered by the enemy. Hand grenades thrown at Japs in jungle fighting were quickly spotted and tossed back, upon occasions. This camouflage treatment was pointed out as being particularly hazardous since the grenades were fully loaded. In the center of the work area was a bomb pit, banked with sandbags, into which the workers have been instructed to toss any grenades on which the firing pins might be accidentally pulled during handling....

Included in S.O.D.'s thousands of employees is a police and guard force of more than 250, including many women; a complete fire department; a railroad system for all hauling within the area limits, into which private carriers are not allowed; a large administration force, and a mail system which handles four truckloads of mail a day.

> *The parking area outside the main gate was jammed with 10 rows of parked cars—each row extending more than two city blocks in length.*[171]

Another reporter described his impression of a visit to the depot to learn "what the Army is doing with the country's cash to win the global war" as follows:

> *The folk living on the outskirts of the depot consider themselves just about as safe as before the depot, with its millions of pounds of explosives, existed. Hundreds of them work there, handle the bombs and shells and they know from experience that they are comparatively harmless at S.O.D.*
>
> *Colonel Elliott and his aides, however, have taken all precautions to provide safety on the shores of Seneca Lake. Major Vacca, provost marshal, has three fully equipped fire houses at the depot. Augmenting the pumpers and brushfire fighters is a tank car that is hauled by a diesel engine to supply additional water if needed…*
>
> *Colonel Elliott admitted that one of his problems has been that of absenteeism, the same as in privately operated industries. He has found that this has been cut down by a six-day rather than a seven-day work week, he said. And he is working for greater efficiency even on the six-day, 'round-the-clock shifts.'*[172]

VARIOUS KINDS OF DEPOT ACTIVITY DURING WORLD WAR II

The depot's mission was the receipt, storage, maintenance and supply of ammunition. As a filler depot, it also issued and reconditioned ammunition for the First and Second Service Commands and for the Boston Port of Embarkation. This included all classes of ammunition and explosives, except chemical ammunition.

There were demolition pits that served as the grounds for conducting ammunition disassembly, detonation and burning. This included numerous types of ammunition, components, guided missiles and explosives. An explosive scrap furnace supported the detonation operation at the site. The burn pads functioned as the burning area for ammunition and ordnance contaminated material such as bulk explosives, pyrotechnics, artillery projectiles, fuses, machine gun ammunition and projectiles using TNT. The nine burn pads were identified as A–L. Pads G and J were used for trash containing contamination from propellants, explosives and pyrotechnics. The demolitions pits and burning pads together comprised ninety acres of demolition area.

There was an Explosive Ordnance Disposal (EOD) that detonated conventional ammunition and explosives weighing less than five pounds. Nearby the EOD were the Ammunition Disassembly Plant buildings.

Surveillance laboratory activities operated in buildings 17 and 18. Throughout the war, inspectors determined the suitability of ammunition, ammunition components and explosives for storage and issue. Nearby the surveillance laboratory were bundle ammunition packing buildings.

The original popping plant, Building S311, was built during 1942 and 1943. The abandoned deactivation furnace was located there. The furnace of the popping plant processed fired brass or steel cartridge cases and a temperature of 1,400 degrees Fahrenheit. Cartridge cases having alive primer were popped and rendered inert.

During 1941 through 1943, several warehouse buildings were constructed. These buildings stored general supplies and possibly small-arms ammunition. The small arms storage building, Number 333, dated back to 1941. Ordnance repair shops were constructed from 1941 to 1943 for the maintenance on all depot vehicles and equipment. The Combat Equipment Area, established in 1942, was approximately four and a half acres and was used to store all types of inert material, including Jeeps, command cars, tanks and carryalls, among other things.[173]

Female Workers

As indicated in the newspaper article above, more than six hundred women held jobs at the depot during the war. They were referred to as WOWs—Women Ordnance Workers. There were many female forklift truck operators for work that didn't take them "out into the fields."[174] Many female workers filled clerical-type jobs as well as working in the various warehouse operations. Elizabeth Harding of Seneca Falls was like many young females who went with their girlfriends to work at the Depot because "there were jobs there." She began working in a supply warehouse and later worked in the carpenter shop "pounding nails and pulling nails" for the wooden boxes.[175]

Roger Allerton, who went to work at the depot in December 1943 at the age of seventeen, emphasized that female workers were paid the same as male workers.[176]

Private Industry Also Wanted Female Workers

Although some female workers stayed on at the depot after the war, private industry in Seneca County competed with the depot for female employees. In 1943, Goulds Pumps ran an advertisement for female workers, specifically saying that women should do "as many women have done—get on the production line" so that they would be "contributing to the nation's war effort." The ad described the female workers they were seeking as "average American mothers and homemakers, but with a will and purpose to be

Rosalie Yaw Mayo was very possibly the first female forklift truck operator hired at the depot. She continued to do this work for many years after World War II. *Courtesy of Rose Smith.*

Several housewives in the area watched the skies by day and night to report any "suspicious aircraft" that might be attacking the Seneca Army Depot. *Courtesy of the Geneva Historical Society.*

helpful in this time of crisis." The ad pointed out that many had no machine training and had probably never even seen the inside of a factory plant.[177]

There was fear that the depot would be a logical target of enemy attack, so much precaution needed to be taken. Although they were not depot employees in the normal sense, several housewives in the area took their turns watching the skies for signs of any "suspicious aircraft." There was one instance in which a "suspicious aircraft" was reported to headquarters. What was learned finally was that a plane was trying to find the airstrip at Ithaca in foggy conditions and had made several wide swings back over the Cayuga Lake area to make another approach to the airstrip.[178]

Italian Prisoners of War

Beginning in May 1944, over 260 Italian prisoners of war were employed at the depot—packing tank treads and loading or unloading trucks or railroad cars—and paid wages provided for all POWs according to the

Geneva Convention. These POWs, employed as a military necessity to relieve the shortage of manpower, had been thoroughly screened by military intelligence and determined to be neither pro-Nazi nor pro-Fascist. They had fought in the Ethiopian campaign and other early battles in North Africa. They were willing to work to help end the war so they could go back to their homes in Italy.

These prisoners worked eight to ten hours each day and also cleaned and maintained their barracks. As rewards, they were taken on sightseeing or educational tours, as well as recreational visits, such as a trip to Niagara Falls—always under military supervision. On Sundays, they had visitors who came from all over the United States. The prisoners included engineers, professors, four boxers and an athlete who had been on the 1938 Italian Olympics team. The camp barber had owned four beauty salons in an Italian city. There were 184 such war-prisoner units at sixty stations in the United States. The Italian POWs had been given different status due to acceptance, by the United Nations, of Italy as a co-belligerent in the war against Germany.[179]

The Italian POWs were also bused to the SMS Lodge (the Societa Di Mutuo Soccorso, an Italian heritage organization established in 1904) in Seneca Falls[180] and the Masonic Lodge rooms in Lodi[181] to enjoy dancing on weekend nights. Elizabeth Harding and her sister Mary frequently brought one or two Italian POWs to their parents' home for a "nice Italian dinner." They also kept up a friendship through correspondence with two former Italian POWs.[182]

Putting all of this into perspective, there were some 51,156 Italian prisoners of war that were brought to the United States. Counting prisoners of war from Germany, Italy and Japan, there were some 425,806 POWs in the United States by the end of June 1945. By June 30, 1946, all but about 147 of these POWs were repatriated. By April 1945, these POWs were at 150 base camps and 340 branch camps throughout the United States.[183] Approximately 90 percent of the Italian POWs agreed to support the U.S. war effort by joining what became known as Italian Service Units. These POWs were then relocated to coastal and industrial sites across the United States and worked with American civilians and military personnel in combat-related work for the remainder of the war. Besides earning money for their work, they were given increased freedom of movement. It was not unusual for Catholic parishes to arrange to host dinners where Italian Americans could meet and visit with these Italian POWs. A documentary titled *Prisoners in Paradise* traces the journey of six young Italians from their entry into the war, through their internment as POWs, to their ultimate marriages with American women after the war.[184]

Local Men Formed Sunday Work Group to Help Speed Depot Shipments

A February 14, 1943, newspaper article reported that a "number" of Seneca Falls men would be spending their Sundays loading ammunition at the depot to help maintain the round-the-clock shipments needed. These men were not depot employees but volunteered to do this work and be paid the prevailing wage. Depot Commanding Officer Colonel Arthur D. Elliott praised their work, saying, "I can't help but be impressed with the sincerity of these men in their desire to help speed the shipment of munitions to our fighting fronts. I am sure that with their help shipments from Seneca Ordnance will materially increase." These Seneca Falls volunteers worked together as a group, traveled to their jobs together and ate together. Their group production was specifically kept track of.[185]

Depot Workers Bought Lots of War Bonds

On May 31, 1943, Congressman John Taber participated in a Minute Man flag-raising ceremony at the depot. This was part of the official government recognition of the fact that more than 90 percent of the employees at the depot were investing 10 percent of their earnings in war bonds. The Seneca Ordnance Depot was one of the first Ordnance Department establishments in the country to receive this award. Seneca depot employees in the previous twelve months had almost 100 percent participation, with in excess of 11 percent of their earnings invested in these war bonds.[186]

Bomb Demolition Work Sometimes Alarmed Area Residents

A common happening at the depot was the detonation of defective ammunition. There was a specific site for this work to take place. Sometimes this detonation caused so much noise and vibration that area residents became alarmed. One of the most serious examples of this was described in the following newspaper article:

> *Seneca County residents learned something of the power of American made bombs this week, when demolitions at Seneca Ordnance Depot caused tremors which shook houses and buildings. Detonation of defective ammunition was carried out by Depot officers, under orders from the War Department, on Sunday, Monday and Tuesday morning. The work was discontinued Tuesday noon, when it was reported that serious damage to brick buildings in the area would result if the explosions continued.*
>
> *The ammunition that was disposed of was defective and not suitable for shipment to combat areas. The demolishing was carefully supervised and was done in an isolated section of the Depot reservation. The ammunition was exploded in relatively small quantities. Ordnance officers said, "The underlying rock strata carried the vibrations, caused by the explosions, as much as 35 miles from the Depot." Brick structures were particularly affected, it was reported.*
>
> *No serious damage was reported in Seneca Falls. Dishes and glassware were knocked from shelves by the tremors and putty was knocked from windows throughout the area. Large windows were particularly vulnerable and plans were being made to bolster the large stained glass window in the Baptist Church when it was announced that the work would be stopped...*[187]

The Manhattan Project

Approximately two thousand barrels of uranium pitchblende,[188] as part of the Manhattan Project, were stored in igloos E0801 through E0811 on the south end of the depot.[189] Depot employee John Stahl spoke specifically of the first box of Manhattan Project materials that was brought into the depot. He operated the forklift truck that took this box from the railroad dock to the small igloo where it was to be stored. He remembered thinking at the time that it was odd to him why an item marked "Manhattan" would be coming here to the depot rather than to New York City. He also pointed out that he couldn't start out with this box until all the "big wheels" (high depot command staff) came down to make sure that all regulations were being followed—including a full guard escort.[190]

Celebrating the End of the War

Sirens, fire whistles and bells celebrated the end of the war on V-J Day in Seneca County on August 14, 1945. Lieutenant General H.H. Campbell Jr., Chief of Ordnance, extended congratulations to all ordnance personnel for the part they played in helping bring about final victory.[191] Hundreds of local men had served in the armed services during the war and hundreds more in industry on the home front.

CHAPTER 6
AFTER WORLD WAR II

After World War II, the Seneca Ordnance Depot was expanded and maintained as a permanent post for storage purposes. In the years immediately following the end of the war, there were large supplies already stored at the depot. There were huge amounts of supplies from the overseas theaters to be brought back to the United States, with many of them shipped to this depot.[192]

HANDLING AMMUNITION

Due to the increase in ammunition returned from overseas after World War II and returns from posts, camps and stations, the army in 1946 built outside storage sheds—known as "X" sites—and outside storage pads for storage of two-thousand-pound bombs and other ammunition. In January 1949, there were 26,480 tons of small arms ammunition of all conditions and grades in outside storage. By 1955, the army sent 737 tons of grade-3 small-arms ammunition and 2,093 tons of twenty-millimeter ammunition into open unprotected storage. In addition to outside storage, the army in 1954–56 constructed a magazine area, buildings 701 through 708, for storing ammunition.

Ammunition inspectors from the Seneca Army Depot (SEAD) regularly sent ammunition, including unserviceable 150-pound bombs in June 1945 and 62,000 high explosive anti-tank mines in April 1946, to

Right: Two soldiers handling a small bomb. Bombs and ammunition of all sizes were handled at the depot. *Courtesy of the Romulus Historical Society.*

Below: Jim Jones of Interlaken checked the lot numbers on a shipment of five hundred bombs that recently returned from Saudi Arabia in 1991. *Courtesy of the* Finger Lakes Times.

DEPOT SALUTE

Finger Lakes Times Special Section — Seneca Army Depot 50th Anniversary — Wed., Aug. 7, 1991

Seneca Army Depot

Jim Jones of Interlaken checks the lot numbers on a shipment of 500 bombs which recently returned from Saudi Arabia. The depot, which covers 10,000 acres, employs about 1,000 people and 500 military personnel. To the bottom left is the logo the

Seneca Army Depot

Pine Camp for demilitarization. (The army redesignated Pine Camp as Camp Drum in 1951 and then as Fort Drum in 1974.)

In 1950, the army constructed ammunition workshops in two locations and SEAD personnel conducted washout, refusing, removal, deboostering

Some shells were being processed in Building 2073. *Courtesy of the Romulus Historical Society.*

and normal maintenance on rocket heads, high explosive shells, fuses and hand grenades. The renovation and demilitarization of ammunition also included surveillance function testing. SEAD personnel sampled test lots of ammunition, including pyrotechnics, establishing the degree of serviceability.

A small-arms range (aka 3.5-inch rocket range) was located on the northeastern portion of SEAD.[193]

Some Other Activities

In July 1955, construction began on a liquid propellant test laboratory, Building 606. Laboratory personnel conducted operational or functional testing of explosive devices. These tests were believed to have occurred on the concrete foundation northwest of Building 606. Starting in 1976, herbicides and pesticides were stored in Building 606. In September 1955, construction began on the fuse storage building.

On June 24, 1958, the Department of the Air Force transferred 622.87 acres of the former Sampson Air Force Base to SEAD. This addition included the five-thousand-foot-long paved runway and the Lake Housing Area.

Soldiers and security guards utilized Range 114 and Building 2302 for shotgun and revolver practice as well as rifle and machine-gun firing. Starting in 1976, the army constructed a skeet and trap range adjacent to the rifle range. In 1981, the army built the Ronald Lee Kostenbader Physical Activity Center, Building 744. The lower level of this building was used as a firing and indoor rifle range.[194]

The Directorate of Supplies

A major function of the depot was to store various kinds of materials and equipment until they were needed by the army. During Operation Desert Storm, for example, large quantities of fence post, barbed wire

Jeeps and many other items needed for a potential war were stored in the General Supply Division warehouse. *Courtesy of the* Finger Lakes Times.

Many items were shipped out of the depot by jet, making use of the airfield acquired from the former Sampson Air Force Base. *Courtesy of Seneca County IDA.*

Large stockpiles of ores were stored at the depot. *Courtesy of the Romulus Historical Society.*

and petroleum products were shipped to the Persian Gulf daily. Nuts, bolts, cots, mattresses and military clothing are other examples of the thousands of general supply items stocked in the directorate's warehouses. "Everything from toothpaste and clothing, to ammunition and heavy mobile equipment was supplied to our soldiers."

In 1973, the directorate took on the additional task of rebuilding the army's industrial plant equipment (what became known as the IPE program). This equipment was owned by the army and included such things as lathes, grinders, presses and boring machines. The machinery was used by the army, or its contractors, to build weapons, ammunition and equipment. The depot rebuilt the entire line of equipment used to produce the M16 rifle. Machines were rebuilt that were used to produce such things as engines and suspension systems for tanks, helicopter engines, gun tubes for tanks and many different types of ammunition. Machines were rebuilt instead of buying new because it saved money to rebuild—benefiting both the army and the taxpayer.[195]

Estimated Replacement Value of this Depot

In 1968, the value of the depot, including the acceptance of Sampson's five-thousand-foot airstrip, exceeded $7 million, with a replacement cost of $90 million. In November 1976, the estimated cost of replacement was over $220 million.[196]

Contribution to the Community

In its years of existence, the Seneca Ordnance Depot contributed significantly to the area. The depot and its personnel consistently took an active role in community affairs. The depot commander often was the keynote speaker at Memorial Day ceremonies in nearby communities, especially Waterloo and Seneca Falls. The depot's fire equipment often helped fight a fire outside the depot itself.

The depot, of course, made a substantial contribution to the local economy. For example, in the fiscal year ending June 30, 1970, the depot spent $14,626,000 for payrolls, supplies, services and other costs. A substantial portion of this amount was spent in the local and Upstate New York area.[197] In 1991, the depot employed about one thousand civilians and five hundred military personnel, with the annual payroll totaling over $46 million.[198] When the salaries are added to the depot's local procurement and utility expenses, it was estimated that the depot pumped over $65 million into the local economy that year.[199]

The property disposal activity carried on at the depot was a secondary source of supply within the Department of Defense and to civilian federal agencies. In the fiscal year ending June 30, 1970, there was a return of materials valued at well over $2 million—savings of taxpayers' dollars. Some organizations that took these "surplus" materials included the veterans' hospitals, federal prisons, Forestry Department, post offices, Office of Economic Opportunity, Agency for International Development and other federal agencies.

The depot had an active donation program. Through the years, millions of dollars' worth of material was released to Girl Scouts, Boy Scouts, Girls and Boys Clubs, Health Education and Welfare (HEW) and civil defense. Through HEW, local schools, hospitals and tax-supported institutions received many items such as vehicles, construction equipment, plumbing supplies and office machines, which reduced community expenditures.

In 1970, the depot was in its sixth year of the president's summer employment youth program, providing work for one hundred young people on vacation from high schools and colleges. While not performing duties ordinarily done by regular employees, the youths assisted in reducing the workload caused by seasonal increases in general clerical tasks and in such diverse areas as brush cutting, painting, window cleaning, reclaiming lumber and lifeguarding.

Each year, for many years, the public was invited to an open house at the depot on Armed Forces Day. There were train and bus tours and general exhibits. Visitors were sometimes taken inside one of the ammunition-storage igloos.

For many years, the Red Cross conducted bloodmobile drives on the depot. The depot was also active in the annual Combined Federal Campaign to raise funds for local and national charitable organizations.[200]

The hamlet of Romulus was fully connected to the depot's water supply service in 1954. This meant that approximately one hundred homes in the town of Romulus and fifty in the town of Varick now had this service. Connection to the depot's sewer system was added in 1979.[201]

Size of the Depot Workforce

In November 1946, the depot employed 595 civilians. At the outbreak of the Korean conflict in June 1950, there were 803 civilians. At the peak of the Korean conflict in July 1952, the civilian workforce totaled 1,821. Following the Korean conflict, the depot employed typically about 300 to 400 military personnel and 600 to 800 civilians.[202] In summer 1970, the depot had a work force of approximately 300 military personnel and 1,004 civilians.[203] In 1991, the Depot employed about 1,000 civilians and 500 military personnel, with the annual payroll totaling over $46 million.[204]

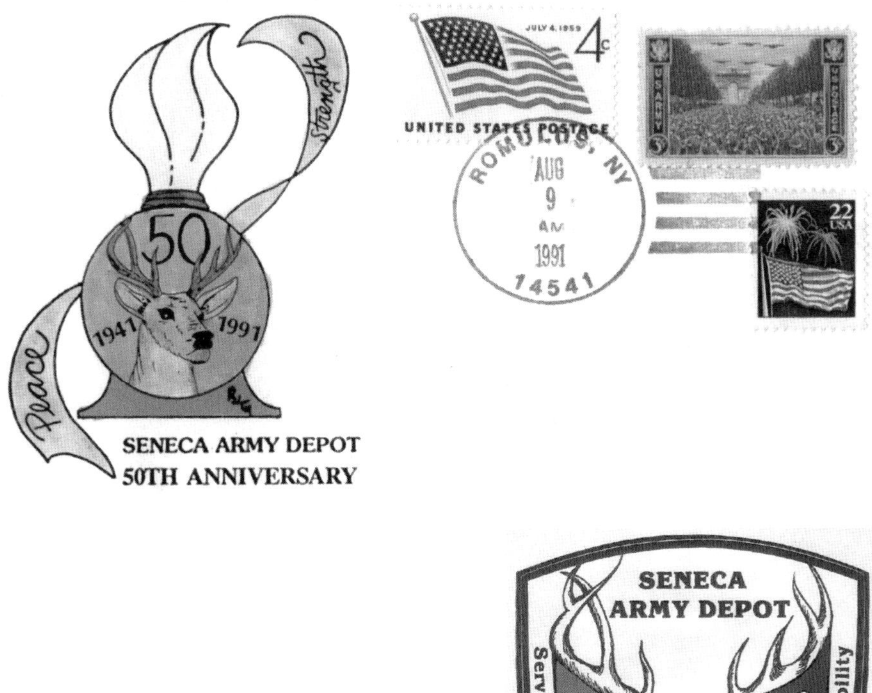

Above: This fiftieth anniversary envelope was used in 1991 mailings. *Courtesy of the Romulus Historical Society.*

Right: This was a frequently used logo, although it was never officially designated as such by the Defense Department. *Courtesy of John R. Zammett Jr.*

"The Last Bomb"

So now we come to an end,
with this bomb we do send.

Our Thanks and regret,
it's really a sure bet.

Seneca's always been the best,
a head above the rest.

With this last round,
Seneca's mission ain't around.

Since 1954, we've done our part,
Our lives we now must restart.

Through our hard work and dedication,
The Cold War has met it's last litigation.

P1, P2 and Lance,
Lord, Please give our lives a chance.

For now we must start anew,
Our careers are up to you.

Even though our bombs will cease,
Let us pray for everlasting peace.

Deep in our hearts we know,
Seneca's put on a good show.

Left: One depot employee, Tom Reynolds, celebrated the handling of the last nuclear bomb at the depot by writing this poem on July 16, 1992. *Courtesy of John R. Zammett Jr.*

Below: This is the last nuclear bomb handled at the Seneca Army Depot. *Courtesy of John R. Zammett Jr.*

The Deer on the Depot

The former Seneca Army Depot today has the largest herd of white deer in the world. When the twenty-four miles of six-foot high steel fence was built around the depot in 1941, several dozen white-tailed deer were probably caught inside the enclosed area. With the fence giving them great protection from natural predators and hunters, the deer population grew rather quickly. Some claimed to have spotted a white deer as early as 1949. The white deer found at the depot are a natural variation of the white-tailed deer, which normally have brown coloring. The white deer are leucistic, meaning they lack all pigmentation in the hair but have the normal brown eyes. (Albino deer lack the pigment melanin and thus have pink eyes.) It is believed that the white deer appeared because of a recessive gene and the protected environment has allowed them to survive.[205]

In 1957, it was estimated there were about 2,000 deer. That year, hunting permits were issued, and 881 deer were shot. None of these could be the growing strain of white deer. The first white fawn was noticed in

The deer herd consists of the typical brown as well as white whitetail deer. *Courtesy of Dennis Money.*

1956,[206] although a *Geneva Times* article of November 1954 talks about a white buck.[207] By 1969, there were 220 white deer leading to a limited number of permits to hunt white deer.

Seneca White Deer, Inc. (SWD) is a 501 c(3) nonprofit organization working to preserve the unique wildlife (especially these white deer) and military history of the former Seneca Army Depot through conservation, ecotourism and economic development. It has periodically conducted bus tours that were almost sold out.[208]

LORAN-C Transmitting Station

Construction of a LORAN-C Transmitting Station was started in 1977 and dedicated on August 2, 1978. This U.S. Coast Guard facility was used by ships and aircraft as far away as one thousand miles to guide them in their flight and navigation. It was the first LORAN-C station to use solid-state components rather than vacuum tubes.[209] This facility went out of use in 2010.[210]

CHAPTER 7
"SPECIAL WEAPONS" AND THE 1983 DEMONSTRATIONS

It is probably safe to say that there were nuclear weapons and/or nuclear weapons components at the Seneca Ordnance Depot for many years. The army referred to them as "special weapons." They were stored at the north end of the depot, hence the origin of the term "North Depot Activity."

North Depot Activity

The North Depot Activity was developed in July 1956. It was widely believed that this area (later referred to as "Q" area) stored "special weapons" (the common army euphemism for nuclear weapons) and their components. It was widely believed that the North Depot Activity stored these "special weapons" for the Griffiss Air Force Base near Rome, New York.[211] In 1961, the North Depot Activity was consolidated with the Seneca Ordnance Depot.

In the early 1980s, it was publicly disclosed that the depot was a major nuclear weapons storage site. The 1982 FOIL documents suggested that the depot was probably the army's largest storage area for nuclear weapons and possible storage site for neutron bombs if they are produced. It was also learned that the uranium for the Manhattan Project (to develop an atomic bomb during World War II) had been stored at the depot before shipment to Oak Ridge, Tennessee. A February 8, 1982 *New York Times*

This recent picture shows evidence today of the tight security around the North Depot Activity area while special weapons were stored there. *Courtesy of Walter Gable.*

This recent photo of the main entrance to the North Depot Activity gives some evidence of the tight security for the Q Area. *Courtesy of Bill Clark.*

Note the special concrete security feature at each corner of the administration building in the Q Area. *Courtesy of Bill Clark.*

To provide security against Soviet aerial spying on North Depot operations, some nuclear weapons components were stored underground beneath what would appear to be a typical building in the Q area. *Courtesy of Walter Gable.*

article said the depot employed 800 civilians and that about 400 troops were stationed there, including 250 military police trained as anti-terrorists and reportedly authorized to kill any intruders approaching the bomb bunkers. These revelations led to anti-nuclear groups picketing the depot. A Women's Peace Encampment set up its residence on a farm just north of the village of Romulus in late July 1983. That summer nearly twelve thousand women visited the encampment and demonstrated against the deployment of the Pershing II and Cruise missiles to sites in Europe.[212]

THE OFFICIAL DEFENSE POSITION

The United States Government (Department of Defense) has basically never officially acknowledged that any kinds of nuclear weapons have been stored at the Seneca Depot at any time. The standard response of the army when asked about the presence of nuclear weapons at the Seneca Depot was: "It is the policy of the Department of Defense to neither confirm nor deny the presence of nuclear weapons at a particular location." It is common for public affairs officers to talk about "special weapons missions." "It's a euphemism that came up years and years ago when people didn't want to say 'nuclear,'" says Lieutenant Colonel Mark Foutch, a Pentagon Public Affairs officer.[213]

REASONS/EVIDENCE FOR THE EXISTENCE OF NUCLEAR WEAPONS

A 1981 Rochester newspaper article referred to the existence of nuclear weapons as the "not-so-secret secret about the Seneca Army Depot." The article pointed out that evidence "strongly indicates that the depot is the U.S. Army's major east coast transshipment point for the delivery of nuclear weapons to Europe." That same article added that the "presence of these weapons certainly makes upstate New York a target for any Soviet missile attack."[214]

Information that can be obtained from public documents makes the depot's role in nuclear weapons fairly clear. That evidence includes the following:

- In the early 1940s, the Manhattan Engineer District (the defense agency responsible for the development of the first atomic bomb) stored two thousand barrels of uranium pitchblende ore in eleven ammunition bunkers at the depot. The low-level ore was stored only for a short period of time.
- In 1957, the depot entered the "special weapons" business, according to a manual given to new employees. In 1966, the manual said, "The depot was assigned the distribution mission for special weapons repair parts with responsibility for serving military establishments in CONUS (continental U.S.) and for overseas agencies through the Seneca Army Depot air strip." According to this manual, the depot also retained its mission for distribution of major special weapons items as well as repair parts.
- While the employees manual didn't use the term "nuclear" in connection with the special weapons mission, it did list four "occupational skills" of depot personnel that help define the special weapons function: "nuclear weapons officer," "nuclear weapons assembly technician," "nuclear weapons maintenance technician" and "nuclear weapons electronic specialist."
- A 1975 *Technical Manual on the Transportation of Nuclear Weapons Material* included Seneca in a list of "military first destinations" for the receipt of nuclear weapons and limited life components received from the Atomic Energy Commission (now the Department of Energy, known as the DOE), which manufactured nuclear weapons for the military. "Limited Life Components" are described as "16-gallon drums" containing "nongamma emitting radionuclides," and "neutron generators." These sixteen-gallon drums likely contained tritium, a highly radioactive hydrogen isotope used in nuclear weapons. The gaseous tritium is used in sizeable quantities in the neutron warheads and, because its half-life is relatively short, it must be replaced periodically. The sixteen-gallon drums were shipped to Seneca by air from the DOE's Savannah River plant, near Aiken, South Carolina. The Technical Manual identified only three Army Military First Destinations, and only two of the three had "requirements" for shipping weapons outside the continental United States.

Of those two, only the Seneca Depot had the requirements for distribution to the U.S. Army in Europe, the manual said.

- A July 1980 DOD/DOE planning document also identified Seneca as one of only two army depots that provided "logistics support for Army nuclear munitions," Seneca was the army's east coast transshipment point. This planning document was officially titled the "Long Range Nuclear Weapon Planning Analysis for the Final Report of the DOD/DOE Long Range Resource Planning Group," and was declassified in January 1981.
- The Reagan Administration on August 9, 1981, announced its plans for assembling neutron warheads that could be airlifted to Europe "within a few hours" once a decision was made to put them there. Both the 1975 Technical Manual and 1980 planning document (see above) pinpointed Seneca as the army's only nuclear weapons storage facility with the requirements for quick deployment of weapons to Europe.
- In 1980, at the request of the Air Force, the army extended the airstrip from five thousand to seven thousand feet. The Air Force felt that the expansion was necessary to accommodate the giant C-141 cargo jets that routinely flew in and out of Seneca. The army justified its request for this $3 million expansion project by telling Congress that C-141 access to Seneca must be maintained because "contingency plans require the rapid out-loading and deployment of (deleted) at Seneca in support of war plans."
- In 1981, the army expanded enlisted men's housing at Seneca in order to accommodate the 833rd Ordnance Company, which was redeployed from South Korea in 1978. The 833rd performed a nuclear function in South Korea.
- In 1982–83, the size of the 295th Military Police Company at Seneca was increased from about two hundred to about five hundred. Only military personnel may guard nuclear weapons.
- The special weapons storage area had all the security features referred to in other articles and official testimony on the storage of nuclear weapons: an "exclusion area" surrounded by three chain link fences, perimeter lighting to make intruders more noticeable, the Intrusion Detection System, military guards and posted signs to warn would-be intruders that the "use of deadly

> force authorized."[215] That exclusion area is six hundred acres in size and only a relative handful of the over one thousand people working at the depot were allowed to go there. This Seneca Depot area precisely matched the Pentagon's descriptions of the conditions under which all nuclear weapons must be stored.[216]

Other pieces of evidence can be added to what that 1981 newspaper article provided. These are:

- The issue of nuclear weapons at this depot was labeled "confidential," which is a very low level of security for the DOD.
- There was a major exercise in 1990 to which the media were invited. It was a nuclear weapons accident training exercise.[217]
- While Seneca Depot officials did not confirm the presence there of nuclear weapons, they did freely concede that the installation was "nuclear capable," meaning there were facilities at Seneca for nuclear-weapons storage and protection.
- The Seneca Depot was named in a 1973 Pentagon technical manual on the transportation of nuclear weapons material as a receiver of nuclear weapons components.
- Another Pentagon document listed the Seneca Depot as a "logistics support" site for "Army nuclear mention"—an apparent reference to the depot's airstrip.
- Seneca Depot had an on-base nuclear emergency action plan. Some of its personnel participated in a special psychological screening program designed by the Pentagon exclusively for those working with nuclear weapons.[218]

More About the Types of Nuclear Weapons Possibly at Seneca Depot

There are both strategic (i.e., long-range) nuclear weapons and tactical (theater) nuclear weapons. Tactical weapons are designed for use in battle and are generally smaller, more portable and less powerful than the strategic weapons, which are designed to knock out an enemy's war-making capacity. The army handled only the tactical weapons, meaning the Seneca Depot probably had only tactical weapons.

From the documentation about Seneca, it seems likely that many of the army's several thousand warheads in Europe came through Upstate New York at one time.[219]

Within the exclusion area at Seneca, there were at least sixty igloos like the forty-eight nuclear storage igloos at the navy's nuclear weapons facility at West Loch, near Honolulu, Hawaii. The exclusion area at Seneca contained a 28,000-square-foot temperature and humidity-controlled maintenance building, which was earth-covered like the storage igloos. According to UCS nuclear engineer Gordon Thompson, such a facility was essential to nuclear weapons maintenance because plutonium burns when wet.

The Seneca Depot's Special Weapons Directorate employed between seventy and one hundred persons (including clerical workers) who did special weapons "assembly, disassembly, and maintenance." Army testimony at the 1980 Military Construction hearings said that 210 C-141s had used the depot airfield between 1976 and 1978 and that some of those flights brought (deleted) cargo back from Europe. Also, the size and function of the depot's special weapons directorate meant that it had the capacity to disassemble nuclear weapons returned from Europe, either for maintenance or dismantling.[220]

Major Protests and Demonstrations in 1983

Even though the Defense Department would "neither confirm nor deny" the existence of nuclear weapons at the Seneca Depot, the mounting evidence motivated many people to become involved in one or more protests throughout the summer and fall of 1983. A Women's Encampment for the Future of Peace and Justice became an organizing centerpiece for many women opposed to nuclear weapons. Famous individuals participated in some of the protests that took place. The protests at the Seneca Depot were the first anti-nuclear weapons protests at any U.S. military base. The protests that took place at the Seneca Depot that summer and fall were reported in newspapers throughout the United States.

The Seneca Women's Encampment for a Future of Peace and Justice

The early 1980s public revelations that the depot was a major nuclear weapons storage site led to anti-nuclear and anti-war activists mounting major protests at the facility beginning in 1983. On May 23, 1983, the Seneca Women's Encampment for a Future of Peace and Justice purchased a small farm on Route 96 just north of the hamlet of Romulus. The camp on that former farm formally opened on July 4. The vision statement, taken from the back cover of the encampment handbook, of this organization included the following:

> *Women have played an important role throughout our history in opposing violence and oppression. We have been the operators of the Underground Railroad, the spirit of the equal rights movement and the strength among tribes. In 1848 the first Women's Rights Convention met at Seneca Falls giving shape and voice to the 19th century feminist movement.*

Women scaling the depot fence during an 1983 anti-nuclear weapons demonstration. *Courtesy of the* Rochester Democrat and Chronicle.

> *Once again the women are gathering at Seneca—this time to challenge the nuclear threat at its doorstep. The Seneca Army Depot, a Native American homeland once* [nurtured?] *and protected by the Iroquois, is now the storage site for the neutron bomb and most likely the Pershing II missile and is the departure point for weapons to be deployed in Europe. Women from New York State, from the United States and Canada, from Europe, and indeed, from all over the world are committed to nonviolent action to stop the deployment of these weapons.*
>
> *The existence of nuclear weapons is killing us. Their production contaminates our environment, destroys our natural resources, and…our human dignity and creativity. But the most critical danger they represent is to life itself. Sickness, accidents, genetic damage and death. These are the real products of the nuclear arms race. We say no to the threat of global holocaust, no to the arms race, no to death. We say yes to a world where people, animals, plants, and the earth itself are respected and valued.*[221]

There were many different people and organizations involved in the planning and running of the Seneca Women's Peace Encampment. The policy of the encampment was to not single out any specific women for their efforts in the organization of or the running of it. Rather, it was a collective effort. The main organizations were the Women's International League for Peace and Freedom, Catholics against Nuclear Arms, the War Resisters League, Women Strike for Peace, Women's Pentagon Action, Rochester Peace and Justice and the Upstate Feminist Peace Alliance.

The encampment attracted thousands of women from many different places and with different political views, sexual orientations, religions, ethnicities and economic backgrounds. While many males shared in the encampment's cause, males were not allowed to join the encampment, though they could be on the front lawn of the encampment.[222]

The July 30, 1983 Incident at Waterloo Bridge

Not surprisingly, the encampment did not integrate well with the surrounding conservative community.[223] An early manifestation of this was apparent in the so-called Waterloo Bridge Incident on July 30, 1983. That Saturday, several women from the New York City Women's Pentagon

Action had started out on their walk from Seneca Falls to Waterloo to the encampment at Romulus. No parade permit was needed, but they had written a letter to the Seneca County sheriff informing him of these plans. The walk was without incident until the marchers' path was blocked at a bridge on Washington Street in Waterloo. A large group of local residents blocked the road. The women marchers sat down on the road. The standoff lasted for some time as the sheriff tried to convince the marchers to give up their march. When many women continued to refuse to leave the road, many of the female marchers were charged with disorderly conduct and taken into custody. One local woman, Mrs. Melley Kleman, felt that those blocking the road, not the marchers, should be arrested and she joined the marchers and was charged as well. A total of fifty-four women were detained, including Mrs. Kleman. They were taken by school bus to the Seneca County Jail, where they were arraigned. Mrs. Kleman was released on bail. The other fifty-three were charged with disorderly conduct and were then taken to the South

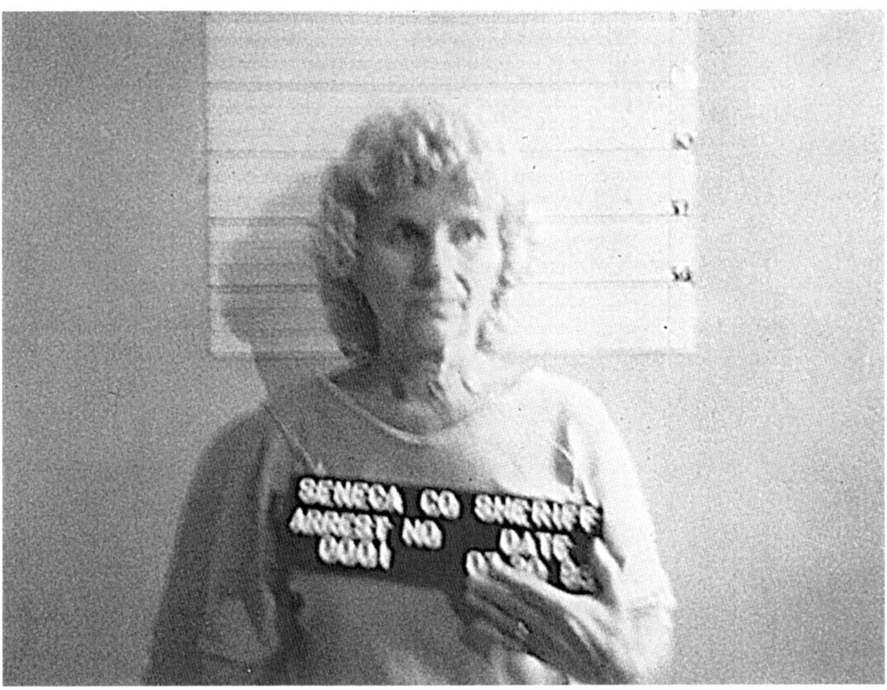

This is the mug shot taken of Mrs. Melley Kleman shortly after her arrest in the incident at the bridge in Waterloo, New York. *Courtesy of Melley Kleman.*

Seneca Elementary School in Interlaken where they were held until the following Wednesday, August 3, 1983.

At that time, the fifty-three were taken to the Waterloo fairgrounds, where they appeared before Waterloo Village Justice Thomas Nessler in a makeshift courtroom in Floral Hall. Judge Nessler dismissed the disorderly conduct charges. The women's fingerprint cards and photographs were returned. They were released to cheering from supporters who had spent the day outside Floral Hall. These supporters had been ejected by Justice Nessler for disrupting the courtroom during his review of the first of the fifty-three cases. Police had to carry some of the women out, and it took forty-five minutes to clear the building. When the proceedings resumed, Seneca County district attorney Stuart Miller read a letter from Stuart Olsowke, chairperson of the Seneca County Board of Supervisors, who recommended that the women be released without bail "in the interest of public safety." District Attorney Miller said that he would not oppose such an action in light of the fact that the women had been jailed for five days and the maximum penalty for the violation is fifteen days in jail. The fifteen defendants, however, that appeared before Justice Nessler each held for dismissal of the charges. Nessler declared a recess at 3:30 p.m. so that he could think about their request. After getting confirmation that he had the authority to dismiss the charges, he decided to do so. "I made what I thought was the best decision," he said.

When Mrs. Kleman was contacted about the dismissal of the charges, she said that she was not satisfied with the dismissal of the charges. "Personally, I wanted to go to trial—I don't feel I was guilty of disorderly conduct," she said.[224]

MAJOR DEMONSTRATIONS THROUGHOUT THE SUMMER AND FALL

Throughout the summer and fall of 1983, a series of major demonstrations took place. Protestors included Bella Abzug, one of the Berrigan brothers and Dr. Benjamin Spock. On three occasions—July 4, August 1 and November 3,1983—feminist artist Helene Aylon covered a section of the fence surrounding the depot with women's pillowcases that in 1982 were filled with "rescued earth" from nuclear sites across the country.[225]

Demonstrations like this took place frequently throughout the summer and fall in 1983. *Courtesy of Robert Zemanek Jr.*

Robert Zemanek Jr. was the public relations director at the Seneca Army Depot throughout the 1983 demonstrations. In a March 2011 interview, he pointed out that the demonstrations that year cost the government about $2 million in additional security expenses and other costs. He pointed out with pride that there was not even one single instance of reported mistreatment coming out of all those protests that year. In that same interview, he commented, "A few of the women [at the Women's Encampment] were reasonable but the majority weren't. It was almost impossible to have rational discussion." He added that people should read *Nuclear Summer* (Louise Krasniewicz, published by Cornell University Press in 1992), which is an anthropologist's study of how the women acted in this group effort. "Twelve thousand women came that summer to demonstrate," Zemanek said.

One of the most widely reported demonstrations took place on October 22, 1983. Approximately 380 protesters were detained that day because they climbed the fence surrounding the depot. A famous member of those detained was Dr. Benjamin Spock, the well-known pediatrician, who was eighty years old at the time.[226] On the day that Dr.

Spock would ultimately get arrested, Bob Zemanek had this interesting story to tell. One of his assistants told him that some woman wanted to talk with Bob as soon as possible. When Bob spoke to this woman, she identified herself as Dr. Spock's wife. She said that her husband was too old to climb over the fence to commit his act of civil disobedience and that she was asking that the fence be opened up, or something else done, so that he wouldn't have to climb over the fence to commit his act of civil disobedience. Bob said that no special accommodations were going to be made. So, what actually happened was that people helped Dr. Spock to climb over the fence.

Cynthia Green of the Associated Press reported, "Dr. Benjamin Spock was handled with care…Spock was among more than 380 people arrested as they climbed a chain-link fence surrounding the Seneca Army Depot in Romulus, N.Y. The famed 80-year-old baby doctor, who wore a tie bearing red peace symbols, was helped over the 6-foot barricade by two women and eased down the other side by two military policemen." She quoted Dr. Spock as saying, "I was a little bit nervous about whether I'd fall flat and look ridiculous." Green went on to report,

> *State police Superintendent Donald O. Chesworth said about 400 protestors blockaded each of the 13 principal gates at the facility…and is believed by nuclear weapons opponents to be the most likely point of departure for Europe-bound missiles. But the blockade had little effect on the operations of the facility and was over by noon, a spokeswoman said.*
>
> *The Seneca protesters, who came from as far away as Indiana and California, were confronted by about 50 flag-waving counter-demonstrators who accused them of being communists, and about 20 hymn-singing evangelists.*[227]

Taking more information from Robert Zemanek's interview in March 2011, we learn something else about that October protest day. In his interview, Bob Zemanek reported that the day began with a heavy fog. He went to work early that morning. He was well aware that the protesters intended to block the depot gates and "close the place down." He told the workers to go to whatever gate would be open—if the women protestors blocked one gate like the main gate, some other gate farther south would be opened. The Women's Camp reported that day they had shut down the depot in that the workers were unable to get in to work. When the depot commander heard that was being said by the media, he ordered that a formal "count" be done of how many workers were actually working that day. The count showed that there actually were more workers present that day than on a normal day.

Some More Recent Information

While the Department of Defense and the Seneca Army Depot never "confirmed nor denied" the existence of nuclear weapons at the depot, there were new reports of their existence at this facility. In June 1985, a new book titled *Nuclear Battlefields: Global Links in the Arms Race*, claimed that there were more than 1,200 nuclear warheads stored at the depot. The book went on to claim that New York ranked second only to South Carolina in the total number of nuclear weapons stored in a state at that time. In addition to the nuclear warheads at the Seneca Depot, the book reported that the depot also had fifty 155-milimeter artillery projectiles, ninety Nike Hercules warheads and sixty atomic demolition munitions, such as land mines. Raymond Zajac, who was the supervisor for the Town of Romulus at the time, commented that he was not surprised to learn about what was reported in the book. He added that he was confident that the army has taken precautions to ensure safe storage of any weapons at the depot. "Certainly the government," Zajac said, "won't jeopardize the welfare of the installation or of the people in the area." Also asked to comment on the book's revelations was Michelle Crone of the Women's Encampment. Her response included that the book "gives us a little boost to validate our presence here. We're going to stay and be vocal and say we cannot afford to have this kind of existence of nuclear weapons in our backyards."[228]

CHAPTER 8
BASE CLOSURE

The end of the Cold War about 1990 set the stage for the ultimate closure of the Seneca Army Depot in July 2000. For a depot that played such an important role supplying army forces in several wars from World War II through the Persian Gulf War, base closure became a real possibility in the early 1990s. The "special weapons" at the North Depot Activity were removed. The special military police that had been providing security also were removed. Speculation arose that the Seneca Army Depot was no longer "necessary."

The end of the "special weapons" North Depot Activity didn't mean that the other kinds of depot operations, such as its extensive IPE (Industrial Plant Equipment) mission had to end here at the Seneca Depot. The army was transitioning, however, to a smaller operation. The Defense Base Realignment and Closure Act of 1990 had provided the basic framework for the transfer and disposal of military installations closed during the base realignment and closure (BRAC) process. It was basically designed to avoid the politics of a member of Congress trying to save a military facility in his/her congressional district or state from closure. The BRAC commission would devise a list of bases for closure and send that recommendation to the president. The president would then forward it to Congress for approval or rejection as a whole package. There were BRAC commission recommendations for base closures in 1991 and 1993 under this new legislation.

Avoiding Unilateral Closure by the Army

The army basically had decided to shut down the Seneca Army Depot without going through the BRAC process. Seneca Depot employees and many local residents, including many in the city of Geneva, were not about to let that happen without a fight. Depot employees organized Keep Our Base at Romulus Alive (KOBRA). Local residents organized Save Our Seneca (SOS). In September 1991, KOBRA and SOS organized a march from the Seneca County Office Building to People's Park in Seneca Falls to help raise the community's awareness of how serious a possibility was total depot closure. In December 1991, SOS got the Seneca County Board of Supervisors to pass a resolution extending an invitation, along with the Geneva City Council, for James Courter, the head of the Defense Base Closure and Realignment Commission, to

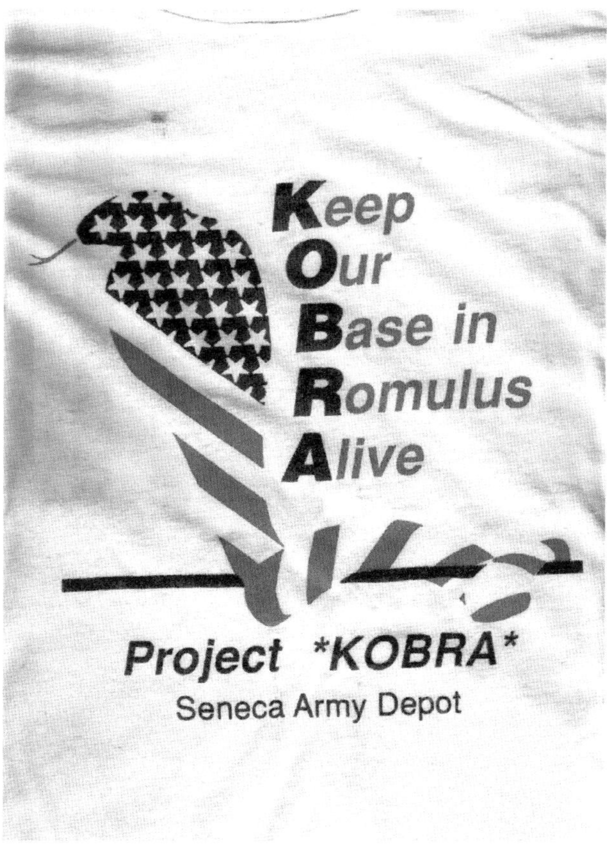

Members of KOBRA wore these t-shirts to show their support for efforts to keep the Seneca Depot open. *Courtesy of John R. Zammett Jr.*

come to the area and meet with SOS in their quest to save the Seneca Army Depot. Approximately $36,000 was raised through donations to hire the Harter, Secrest and Emory law firm in Rochester to seek an injunction claiming that the army had shut down the depot's two largest missions—Special Weapons and Industrial Plant Equipment—without a review by the Base Realignment and Closure Commission. At the hearing on whether to grant the injunction, Federal Judge David G. Larimer in Rochester seemed rather amazed that the army lawyers were not able to provide the information that the judge wanted. The judge tabled the injunction request. About a month later, the judge granted the injunction, in effect ordering the army to follow the BRAC process regarding downsizing or closure of the Seneca Depot.[229]

That did not mean, however, that the Seneca Depot would stay open. As Michael Lambert, the union president at the time, said, "The Army had arbitrarily decided that it was going to close the base. We thought it was the lesser of two evils for the Depot to undergo the BRAC process rather than have the Army arbitrarily end the employment of all the Depot workers."

After corresponding with the BRAC committee only a few times, union leaders soon became convinced that the BRAC committee really didn't know everything they needed to know about the Seneca Depot. According to Michael Lambert, they didn't know that Seneca Depot had an airfield, the total warehouse storage capacity or much in general about the existing infrastructure of railroads and storage igloos. Lambert said, "We corresponded with the BRAC Committee at least three to five times a week, giving them updates of our infrastructure. There were certain criteria that we had to meet—like rocket and ammunition maintenance, etc.—that demanded certain facilities. We had it all at our depot basically; very little more would have to be built to meet all the criteria."

It was the decision of the BRAC committee that the Seneca Depot remain open. The KOBRA and SOS people knew, however, that the political process was going to override any other consideration. They felt that it was either Seneca Depot or the Sierra base in California that was going to be closed. They felt that Sierra had all the political clout compared to Seneca. Congressman Frank Horton, who had been a strong advocate for the Seneca Depot, was no longer the representative for the area that included the depot. The new congressman was Amo Houghton. He had come up a couple times to meet with SOS and

KOBRA, but those groups sensed it was just a "dog and pony show"—that either he wasn't interested in their struggle or that he knew that the decision had already been made.

The 1995 BRAC report provided for the closure of the Seneca Army Depot but not the Sierra Depot. Consistently the evaluations of operations at the Seneca Depot resulted in an overall rating of "outstanding" or "exceptional" while those of the Sierra base were "marginal" at best. So, why was Seneca slated for closure and not Sierra? Was it political clout? Was it simply that Sierra had this one following advantage over Seneca—that in its desert location, it could detonate explosives up to ten thousand pounds in size while Seneca was limited to one hundred pounds?

Implementing the Closure Decision

The 1995 BRAC closure list was accepted by Congress, meaning that the Seneca Army Depot would be closed. In September 1995, 503 civilian employees at the depot received notices that they would be laid off. Bruce Johnson said, "My goal as being the civilian in charge of depot activities from 1995 to 2000 [when formal base inactivation occurred] was to help get anyone eligible for retirement retired before the Depot closed. I was up front about that and am proud of it." It is probably safe to say that union leadership basically agreed with his actions. There were inevitable instances of a particular employee complaining to union leadership that he or she had logical reasons why not him or her instead of someone else—especially given the fact that veterans got an advantage over non-veterans. It is clear that under the BRAC process, affected employees had benefits—expenses for relocation, job retraining, etc.—that they never would have received had the army unilaterally closed the depot. Michael Lambert also pointed out that by following the BRAC process, there was a time period in which several depot employees managed to get in enough time to retire so that they continued to live in the nearby area—thereby continuing to be contributors to the local economy. By gaining that additional time and benefits, less than one hundred employees were involuntarily separated. This was in sharp contrast to the several hundred that would have been involuntarily separated had the army been able to unilaterally close the depot.[230]

Inactivation Ceremony on July 20, 2000

The Seneca Army Depot was officially inactivated on Thursday, July 20, 2000. The inactivation ceremony took place outside Building 101, home of the base commander's office. Lieutenant Colonel Brian Frank relinquished his depot command to Colonel Lawrence Sowa of the Munitions and Armaments Command at Rock Island, Illinois. Sowa called the ceremony a day of remembrance for the sacrifices people made for the depot and the work accomplished there. Depot workers, he said, set the benchmark for ammunition storage and distribution. "In every conflict from World War II to Bosnia, assets from Seneca leveraged our military success on the battlefield and I thank you for it," he said. Sowa also praised Frank for overseeing the depot's final downsizing with dignity and care. Sowa pointed out that in Frank's one year as the depot commander, Frank had supervised the transfer of five hundred pieces of industrial plant equipment and 130,000 tons of ammunition, turned the hazardous materials enclave over to another army agency and conveyed depot property to reusers.

Lieutenant Colonel Brian Frank (center), the depot commander, looks on as the depot flag is being rolled up in the deactivation ceremony held at the Seneca Army Depot on July 20, 2000. *Courtesy of the* Finger Lakes Times.

Glenn Cooke, the executive director of the Seneca County Industrial Development Agency, which was ultimately to receive title to most of the former depot property, credited the successful depot reuse efforts to a strong collaboration between the army and the private sector. "Today is not the end of the story for the Seneca Army Depot," said Cooke. He went on to list how the depot was being redeveloped: housing units that had been taken over by a real estate management company; the maximum security prison which opened in August 2000; the depot's airfield's transformation into a law enforcement training facility; and the sale of warehouse space to PEZ Lake Development, which that morning was trucking in its first load of storage material.

Attending this inactivation ceremony was Edward Montford, age eighty-five. He had with him a July 22, 1941 letter from the U.S. War Department that instructed him and his wife, Emily, to leave their Varick farm in three days. They had been married for about a year and were farming on 120 acres. They were in the midst of harvesting and quickly moved their animals to a small "run down" farm near Stanley in Ontario County.[231]

Finger Lakes Times Article Gave Historical Summary of the Seneca Army Depot

On June 21, 2000, the *Finger Lakes Times*, a Geneva-based daily newspaper that serves the greater depot area, carried this historical summary of the Seneca Army Depot:

> *On June 11, 1941, the War Department approved building an $8 million munitions project in central New York after studying 61 locations around the country. A total of 10, 923 acres of farmland belonging to 195 families in Seneca County were purchased.*
>
> *Army historical documents say the area was selected because of the suitability of the land and its proximity to the Atlantic coast. Also, records say the War Department was impressed with the availability of "preponderantly good American stock of the area" from which a workforce could be drawn.*

> *Between Aug. 21 and Nov. 13, 1941, workers constructed nearly 500 ammunition storage igloos while also setting up nearly 20 miles of fence surrounding the site to seal it off from the public.*
>
> *The depot's civilian employment peaked in July 1943 when 2,500 employees worked at the site. That figure dropped to 595 by the end of World War II.*
>
> *By September* [2000], *the depot's workforce will be down to 11 employees, primarily as caretakers.*
>
> *Originally established as an ammunition supply and storage depot; in recent years the depot's mission has involved receiving, storing, caring for and maintaining conventional ammunition and general supply items, which include hazardous materials.*
>
> *The Army estimates that if a similar facility were to be built today, the cost would be about $850 million.*[232]

On September 30, 2000, the Seneca Army Depot was formally closed and moved to a caretaker status. The depot had been downsized from 1,200 employees to just 7.[233]

CHAPTER 9

AFTER THE CLOSURE OF THE DEPOT

The inactivation of the Seneca Army Depot meant that the army would be turning over portions of the former Seneca Army Depot to the Seneca County Industrial Development Agency (IDA). Not all was transferred immediately. The initial transfer was just over 1,100 acres. On September 30, 2003, about 7,000 acres of the former Seneca Army Depot were transferred to the IDA. The county's Industrial Development Agency and its Economic Development Corporation continue to seek uses of this property for the economic viability of the county. The delay in transfer of these acres and other acres has been due to the environmental clean up of portions of the depot. A small acreage has still not been transferred to the Seneca County IDA, as of August 1, 2012.

The Seneca County Industrial Development Agency is a public benefit corporation dedicated to ensuring the long-term economic health of Seneca County by attracting new businesses and helping existing businesses grow. The agency promotes private sector commercial and industrial development, and advances the job opportunities and economic welfare of the people of the county.[234]

The current executive director is Robert J. Aronson. Patricia A. Jones is the deputy director.[235] IDA board members are Thomas L. Kime (chair), G. Thomas Macinski, Robert E. Kernan Jr., Robert J. Rosenkrans, Patricia Amidon, Kenneth Reimer, Michael Hrysak and Steven Brusso.[236]

Installation Restoration Program

Since 1978, the Seneca Army Depot has been participating in the Installation Restoration Program (IRP). Under this program, the Defense Department has identified, investigated and cleaned up much contamination from hazardous materials. The depot's demolition of munitions for forty years had consisted of open burning of fuses, projectiles, explosives and propellants directly on the ground surface. This is a primary reason why portions of the former depot are still on the National Priorities List (of the most hazardous sites across the United States and its territories) of the U.S. Environmental Protection Agency Superfund. In its Internet site update of August 9, 2012, the EPA Superfund Site Progress Profile for the Seneca Army Depot shows that current human exposure at this site is under control and that contaminated ground water migration is under control. There is still some clean-up taking place on the former depot, but the vast majority of the acreage is considered "ready for anticipated use."[237]

KidsPeace and Hillside Children's Center

Prior to the actual closure, plans were underway to find alternative uses for the deport area. One such alternative in a northern portion of the property was the KidsPeace Seneca Woods Campus. Seneca Woods Campus was opened in 2000 to treat as many as 1,200 New York children who previously were sent out-of-state for specialized treatment. At the campus there was a residential program for children with clinical emotional problems and history of delinquency, educational/vocational training and a comprehensive after-care program consisting of supervision and support networks. In December 2004, the Seneca Woods Campus of KidsPeace was taken over by Hillside Children's Center. The center provides residential housing and treatment for youth suffering from mental health or behavioral challenges. At the writing of this book, the Hillside Campus had over 350 employees.

Five Points Correctional Facility

The Five Points Correctional Facility, a New York State prison, is located at the extreme south east end of the former depot property. This 750-cell facility opened in summer 2000 and has created over 650 new permanent jobs.

Depot Airfield

This five hundred-acre parcel includes a seven-thousand-foot runway. The New York State Police have a presence at this site at the New York State Police and Fire Training Center. In addition, a fire tower was constructed at this site and is used by local fire departments in training their volunteer firefighters.

Seneca County Law Enforcement Center

The new Seneca County Law Enforcement Center was built on the depot in 2006 and is considered a state-of-the art facility. This facility houses the county sheriff's department as well as the county jail. Employment at this facility exceeded 130 personnel in August 2012.

Finger Lakes Technology Group, Inc.

A subsidiary of the Ontario and Trumansburg Telephone Companies, the Finger Lakes Technology Group, Inc. (FLTG) is a telecommunications provider with a twenty-year lease agreement to a portion of the former Seneca Army Depot's conservation area. This depot site is a network monitoring station for companies worldwide and serves as a data backup storage site. The company is converting some sixty-four former igloo bunkers to serve as impenetrable storage areas for various companies to have an off-site facility for data backup and recovery. In addition, these former munitions igloos will be available to companies for equipment storage and for secure storage of such materials as papers, records,

An aerial view of igloos. *Courtesy of Bill Clark.*

tapes and cabinets. Starting in 2008, FLTG provided expanded and enhanced internet and telecommunications services for several area school districts.[238]

Seneca Depot, LLC

Seneca Depot, LLC, is currently leasing the Depot Planned Industrial Development (PID) and warehouse areas. The Advantage Group (TAG), a tenant of Seneca Depot, LLC, is currently utilizing numerous buildings in this area for the refurbishment and storage of restaurant equipment. TAG employs approximately thirty employees at this writing.

Fort Drum Soldiers Conduct Training Exercises

The Seneca County IDA approved a request from Fort Drum to conduct training exercises at the former depot in summer 2008. The training was to consist of simulated ammunition or paint ball–like materials, HumVees and helicopters. The training was to include driving, air operations, combat operations, life support operations and escape and invasion. In January 2011, the IDA extended the license agreement for two more years. More than three hundred members of the Ninety-first Military Force Battalion were involved in training exercises in March 2011. The training area was about three thousand acres.[239]

The First Baptist Church of Romulus (i.e. "Kendaia Church") and Cemetery

When the Seneca Ordnance Depot was established in 1941, the War Department acquired ownership of the property of the First Baptist Church of Romulus and its cemetery. As this church was located near the hamlet of Kendaia, local folk referred to this church as the Kendaia Church.

The church had been constituted in June 1795 with seven members. This was possibly the first church organized in what is today Seneca County. William Watts Folwell donated a lot in 1808 for the erection of a meetinghouse. By 1849, the church building was in such a state of decay that south winds would blow open the church doors, allowing cattle to enter the building. Alterations were made to the church building. The building was moved a little to the south and an eight-foot-wide portico with four columns was added to the east. The church sanctuary or auditorium was relocated to the second floor, with the lower floor to be used for group meetings and entrance. This remodeling made the appearance of the church basically what it looks like today.[240]

The cemetery was located on the north side of the church. Later the cemetery expanded to the south side as well. Within the cemetery are buried at least four Revolutionary War veterans, as well as veterans of virtually every war since the Revolution.

When the properties were acquired for the depot, the army promised that the cemetery would continue to exist—that burials could still take place on the family plots and that family members would be able to visit gravesites. The army kept that promise. Throughout the years of existence of the Seneca Army Depot, burials took place at this cemetery. Since the closure of the depot in 2000, the cemetery association has continued to maintain the cemetery. Any interested person has been allowed to visit

Walter Gable, Gail Snyder and Naomi Brewer are shown with the wreath placed at the Kendaia Cemetery on May 29, 2011, to help pay tribute to the army's keeping its promise that this cemetery would continue to exist and that family members would have access to their family burial plots. *Courtesy of Carolyn Zogg.*

the cemetery on the Sunday of Memorial Day weekend. Burials take place on family lots. On May 29, 2011, the local historians who planned the events marking the seventieth anniversary of the establishment of the Seneca Army Depot gathered at the cemetery to place a commemorative wreath. In his remarks on behalf of the that group, Seneca County historian Walter Gable pointed out that the army kept its promise that this cemetery would continue to be a functioning cemetery.

The fate of the church building itself is a sadder story. The last church service was held on Sunday, September 7, 1941. An overflow crowd of more than one hundred residents attended. The *Geneva Daily Times* reported, "Outside, in closely parked rows, Model T Fords sat comfortably beside handsome new automobiles. Inside, elderly couples mingled with the youth of the church, the ties of grief binding them together. Handkerchiefs were often in view as memories went back over the past." Historian Dean Bruno reported that while the final service was a time of sadness, the parishioners made a special effort to remember the pioneering spirit of their ancestors and also acknowledge the sacrifice that family, friends and neighbors were making in the name of national defense. Local resident Paul Baldridge wrote a poem, "Patriots of '41," that was read during the service. The final two stanzas showed how the people of Seneca County had endured much as frontier settlers in an area of great agricultural potential:

I give you men of forty-one
An uncompelling kind,
A proud unyielding race of folk
With purpose set and mind;
A pioneering, forward breed
Inured to loss or gain,
Too proud to turn from charted course,
From snow or sun or rain.

I give you men of sky and sod,
Of furrows straight and long,
Of bulging barns and fatted kine,
Of thankfulness and song;
I give you folk of sacrifice
In name of freedom done
Whose trek afar an epic makes
In nineteen forty-one.[241]

Early on in the construction of the depot, the church building was used for storage and a break room for the construction workers. In the mid-1950s, the church building was bought, dismantled and removed to Irelandville northwest of Watkins Glen, where it still stands today. G. LaVerne Freeman was buying up old buildings to establish Old Irelandville (which was later called York Yankee Village) as a tourist attraction. It was to be a typical village of the post–Civil War period. As the Kendaia Baptist Church was being taken apart, each piece was carefully marked for reconstruction. Tragically, as the church structure was being reconstructed, a severe wind blew apart some of the structure and a heavy beam landed on Freeman's head, knocking him out. Freeman, who had a PhD in psychology and had served as a naval officer during World War II, never completed his village. The church building was never used for anything but storage.[242]

There is a sharp contrast in the current status of the Kendaia Cemetery and the church building. The army kept its promise that the cemetery would continue as a functioning cemetery, but a similar promise regarding the church building was never made. The church structure stands virtually neglected about thirty miles away from the former depot. Rather ironically, it still "exists" but not so for the former Seneca Army Depot.

WHAT'S AHEAD?

Interestingly, none of the uses for the former depot property includes returning it to what it was before the depot—farmland. All of this underscores that what is the most important use for a particular area is relative to the needs of the time. In mid-Seneca County in 1941, farmland was deemed less important than a munitions facility for American involvement in World War II. Then came a similar need with the Korean War. Then came a needed storage site for "special weapons" materials during the Cold War. We are still experiencing the post–Cold War era reality that this depot is no longer needed and suitable alternative economic uses need to be found.

ACKNOWLEDGEMENTS

An idea becomes reality when embraced with hard work and enthusiasm. This is what the ad hoc Planning Committee of local historians gave to us in generous abundance. We cannot thank them enough for their guidance, focus and merry spirit—it made this publication live. Thank you to Naomi Brewer, Ovid Historical Society; Allan Buddle, Backbone Ridge History Group; Ann Buddle, Interlaken Historical Society; Sally VanRiper Eller, Romulus Historical Society; Yvonne Greule, Romulus Historical Society; Bill Sebring, Romulus Town Historian; David Smith, Ulysses Historical Society; Gail Snyder, Ovid Historical Society; and John R. Zammett, Jr., former depot employee. We—Walter Gable, Seneca County Historian, chair, and Carolyn Zogg, Lodi Historical Society—were part of this committee.

The Seneca County Industrial Development Agency and the Seneca County Economic Development Corporation sponsored in part, a three-program series, which were hosted by the Ulysses Historical Society, the Seneca Falls Historical Society, the Lodi Historical Society and the Romulus Historical Society.

Professional marketing and advertising help came from Megan Connor Murphy of Dixon Schwable. Thanks to our program presenters: Sally VanRiper Eller, a dispossessed family member; Walt Gable, historian and writer; Bruce Johnson, retired assistant civilian executive officer; Pat Jones, deputy executive director of IDA; Melley Kleman, arrested for her support of the right of women to march in 1983; Robert Zemanek Jr.,

Poster prepared by Dixon Schwable for program series publicity. *Courtesy of the Seneca County IDA.*

retired public affairs officer; Bill Dorn, Finger Lakes Technology Group; Neal Sherman, The Advantage Group; Dennis Money, president of Seneca White Deer, Inc.; and Bob Aronson, executive director of IDA. We thank John Lempke, superintendent of Five Points Correctional

Facility, for its special exhibit; the Seneca County Board of Supervisors for funding the historic marker denoting the years and activities of the Seneca Army Depot. We thank all the individual donors and the Seneca White Deer, Inc. and IESI (Seneca Meadows Landfill) for the funding for another historic marker honoring the dispossessed families. We thank Roy Gates, superintendent; James Rappleye, deputy superintendent; and staff of the Seneca County Highway Department for placing the two markers on Route 96A and Route 96. Thanks to Dean Bruno who was the keynote speaker at the dedication of the dispossessed families marker.

Thanks to Naomi Brewer and Ann Buddle who read and reread chapter proofs with clear vision; Catherine Schunk, attorney; and Frank Fisher, county attorney, who provided us legal advice. We are very grateful to Whitney Tarella, our editor, encouraging and kind, who has wholeheartedly supported our efforts for a written history of the Seneca Army Depot. Many, many helped with refreshments and exhibits, parking and sign making: Gail Snyder, John Zammett, Alan Buddle, Noel Clawson, Philomena Cammuso and Yvonne Greule.

We especially express our gratitude to the *Finger Lakes Times*, Geneva Historical Society and Michael Karpovage.

We thank those who shared at our programs and those interviewed who shared their stories and experiences of the Seneca Army Depot, especially Florence Lisk Vargason, over ninety years old.

Publishing a book and erecting two historic markers has long been a highly desired conclusion to our program series. We thank each and every person who has made this idea become reality.

APPENDIX I
INTERVIEWS OF VARIOUS PEOPLE'S ASSOCIATIONS WITH THE DEPOT

As part of the three-series program on the Seneca Army Depot, many people came forward to tell their story of personal memories while working at the depot. Some of the interviews are included. It is interesting to note the broad range of duties and thoughts experienced by those interviewed.

Roger Allerton

Interviewed by Naomi Brewer and Walter Gable

I started work at the depot in December 1943 when I was only seventeen years old. My twin brother started working there in July 1943. He typically worked six days of the week for ten hours each and then on Sundays for eight hours. I was first paid sixty-seven cents an hour. After thirty days, my pay was raised to seventy-two cents an hour. For some of my employment time, I stayed in the civilian housing behind the old NCO post. I retired from the depot in 1985 and have continued to live in Ovid since then.

There was a company of black soldiers that came to the depot in January 1944. They were just out of basic training and were there for only a short time. They had a hard time with the winter weather and often got frostbite. They worked in Supply as truck drivers. On weekends they went to Pine Camp [Fort Drum] for training. They didn't like going to Pine Camp because it was even colder there. Here at the depot they were in segregated housing—down in the area of the incendiary plant, near the Sampson entrance.

Women worked as forklift truck operators in the dental supply area. Their vehicles were gas-powered. These female workers were paid ninety-two cents per hour, the same as male workers. No women ran any forklifts out in the fields. In the field warehouses—they were used for small weapons—only electric forklift trucks were used to decrease the chances of combustion/explosions. These forklift truck operators were paid eighty-seven cents an hour.

The gang base workers were paid eighty-seven cents per hour. Foremen were paid ninety-two cents an hour.

The Italian POWs were also based down in the area of the incendiary plant near the Sampson entrance. These Italian POWs were paid in coupons and money. They saved the money. They used their coupons to get cigarettes that the regular American workers could not. I would arrange to get cigarettes from some of the Italian POWs. They were very crafty people. Some of these Italian POWs were bused to the SMS club [an Italian fraternal organization] in Seneca Falls. When the Italian POWs were bused to see Niagara Falls one day, several American workers got upset about this special treatment.

There was a work order to prepare a shipment of Studebaker trucks parts loaded in crates to go to Russia. Red stripes were to be painted onto the crates. It was during the winter and not suitable weather conditions for painting on these red stripes. Commander Elliott ordered that all of Shop 2 would be used until this mission was completed. Shop 2 had direct rail line access.

In 1942, munitions were being transported from the railroad cars to the igloos by women driving flatbed-like Mack trucks. One of the first such women workers was Peggy Glenn, of Waterloo, who is now deceased. After first using these Mack trucks, they changed to using trailer trucks.

All kinds of items were brought to the depot after the end of World War II. Everything was mixed up. There were various X sites that looked like poll barns for the storage of these items.

I still have my original worker badge. Those early worker badges had basically just a safety pin clasp, and they could easily come off. I lost my original badge and was issued a new one. Someone then found my original badge, and I just kept it. My badge included my employee number with the letter "Z." This letter was added to indicate that I was not yet eighteen years of age. From these original badges, there was a change to using color-coded badges. Yellow was used for administration, red for magazine employees, orange for general supply workers and blue for utilities/engineers. This color-coding made it much easier for security force employees to determine if a worker were in some work area not authorized to that worker.

In the warehouses, there was a warehouseman, gang boss and the crews. Everything in the warehouses had to be counted, and clipboards were used to write the item, their number, weight, quantity in each box and any information. It was cold in there, and I felt sorry for an older woman. The women had to wear gloves, and it was so hard to count items and write.

Warehouse 333 was the only one with steel doors. It was loaded with shotguns, carbines, sub machine guns, forty-five-caliber pistols and all kinds of weapons, all in boxes. It was top security. To go in there, you had to sign in and sign out.

BETTY CRANE

INTERVIEWED BY ANN BUDDLE

I began work at the Sampson Naval Base, Sampson College and Sampson Air Force Base and was transferred to the North Depot of the Seneca Ordnance in 1957, which was in the process of being built. I was the third woman hired. We worked in a warehouse while our offices were being constructed. The warehouse eventually became the commissary. I had top-secret clearance. We had to show our badge at the first gate, turn it in and get another badge to enter the area. I was a senior stock control clerk. We were perhaps ten or twelve women working, some civilian and some military. It was a busy office with typing and handling all the paperwork for the components that were necessary for the mission. I thought these components were probably stored in Q area. In addition, I trained civilian and military personnel in stock control procedures.

Then I was transferred to the Chief Administrative Branch of the Administrative and Planning Office for North Depot activities. I supervised the group maintaining the classified documents related to the North Depot activities. I remember a line of file cabinets, perhaps eight in number, all securely locked. Every morning, I would unlock each file cabinet, supervise the staff of four to eight people doing clerical work, sign out needed documents to personnel, sign the documents back in at the end of the day and once again lock the file cabinets. We were regularly told that once you leave the North Depot area, the workday activity was not to be discussed.

I left the depot in 1963 to marry Merwyn Crane, a widower with five children. Merwyn's parents, Vance and Nellie Crane, had little notice to vacate their farm near what is called Bull's Head, the intersection of Routes 96 and 414. They had a grain and cattle farm, as well as working at Willard Psychiatric Hospital. My in-laws had a chance to harvest their grain before the government took possession of their land. They then moved to the village of Interlaken and kept only their chickens. Eventually, they started the Crane/TV Appliance business.

Anita Fitzgerald

Interviewed by Walter Gable

I really don't know how the Italian POWs started coming to the SMS Lodge—whether the officers at the depot got in touch with the SMS or not. The Italians POWs would come on Saturday nights. There was a lot of hard feelings because many people didn't want any associating with the prisoners. So it didn't last long. There was a lot of resentment of having the prisoners come and have a good time while our soldiers were off to war fighting. Some of the older women really enjoyed it. It was like being back home, talking to someone from Italy. They had come from Italy, and they spoke excellent Italian. It really perked up my Italian.

On Sunday, I would go to visit with the prisoners on the depot property. They were nice gentlemanly people, and they were very accommodating. We would go into the depot off Route 96 where there would be nice picnic tables. The older women would bring baskets of food. If the POWs knew someone had a birthday, they would bake a birthday cake. They were not really young kids; the majority were way over twenty. They were very polite. There was nothing to do except walk around and talk. Some would play cards. We would stay an hour or two. You would go on your own on Sundays. If you met some person, you would go just to see that one man. We girls would go in groups of two or three.

In the group that I was in, there was one prisoner who had seen a local newspaper. He lived on the coast in the Tuscany area. In the paper, he saw this picture of his town being bombed, but he saw his house in the picture. He wondered about his parents, so I wrote a letter. It took about a month for me to get a response back from his parents. I gave the letter to him, and he was glad to learn that his parents were OK. He was also worried about his sister who lived farther south. I found out from the letter from his parents that his sister was OK. When he went back home to Italy, I never corresponded with him.

For a while, there were dances for the prisoners at the SMS Lodge. I never went to them, however.

The Italian POWs were clever. I had this ring that was made from the handle of a toothbrush. The prisoners worked with machinery, and they were cooks. This one made this ring. It was fascinating. It had a picture that was slit into the toothbrush handle. It was a picture of the prisoner who made the ring. They would make different things. They also worked in the laundry and kept the grounds.

My cousin worked at the rations office. The husband of a lady that worked with my cousin was a fireman. When there was some special event on the weekend we would go and have a good time. We would see how the firemen, when needed, prepared to slide down the fire pole.

There was a USO in Seneca Falls. It was located about where the VFW is today. You would sign in and sign out. We went there several times. There was dancing. There were both soldiers and sailors because we had Sampson Naval Station.

Elizabeth Harding

Interviewed by Walter Gable

I went to work at the depot because four of my girlfriends wanted work, and we decided to go to the depot and work together. One of my girlfriends was actually black but very light skinned and with pretty blue eyes. I worked during the war in a supply warehouse. We did things like what you would do in a store—stocking items and waiting on people. The Italian POWs worked in the area, and they would come to the warehouse for supplies. They would talk in Italian, and we didn't let on that we knew what they were saying, for quite some time, until this one time. The one time was when one POW said something bad, and another female worker and I laughed to the point that the POW said he knew that we knew what he had been saying. I didn't admit that I was Italian because I didn't want him to know that I didn't know all of these dialects. My friend did know some of the old dialect because her mother spoke it, and she did help translate some letters. My friend could easily talk with these POWs in Italian, but reading and translating the written dialects was so much more difficult.

After the warehouse, I worked in a carpenter shop pounding and pulling nails for the wooden boxes. We would go into the boxcars and stock, but we didn't have anything to do with ammunition. We would write false phone numbers in the boxcars. I worked swing shift while in the carpenter shop.

About two or three of the POWs regularly came to dinner at my folks. There was a bus that would take them to these places. The POW from near Venice was very good-looking. Anita Avveduti and Vinnie Saracino were also part of our circle—my sister Mary, Anita, Vinnie and me. We didn't go to parties or dances.

I kept contact with Geno Bolzanella and Frank Galella. (Frank is now deceased.) There was a Pietro (Peter) from Rome. He was quite a character…He would get up on the table and sing songs against "Il Duce." Others I knew only by seeing them. Whenever Geno wrote a letter, he always ended his letters by thanking my parents for the wonderful meals that they served when Geno and the other POWs would come to dinner. Mary and I went to Italy to see Geno. Frank married a girl named Ann and came to America to live. My sister Mary went to Italy more than once. I didn't know what Italy was like. The sky was so beautiful. My mother would talk about that, and we girls growing up just didn't believe her. But when I actually visited Italy, I realized how correct my mother was. Mother was from Castelaneta, way down near the heel. Geno was having trouble with his pension, and I helped him out by going to Don Merriam (of the Veterans' Office here in Seneca County) so that Geno could get his pension.

I worked about three years at the depot but stopped when the war was over. With the terrible winter storms, it was difficult to get to and from work.

MICHAEL LAMBERT

INTERVIEWED BY WALTER GABLE

I was employed at the depot from July 24, 1978, until September 1999. I started out as a security guard and then I went to the IPE division. I got a pipefitter apprenticeship for four years and became a journeyman in 1980–1995.When the announcement came that the depot was going to be under BRAC, all trade positions were eliminated. So I was bumped into the ammunition division.

As a workforce, we knew we were what the army was transitioning to—small and versatile. We always had a real positive attitude as far as doing our job. It showed—we always got "outstanding" or "exceptional" on our performance reviews by the army—be it special weapons, supply mission, etc. But we also knew that as a result of our missions that it would play to our undoing as well. The special weapons mission was a secret mission that wasn't well known throughout the army community. When we were corresponding with the BRAC committee that studied small ammunition storage facilities, there were certain facts that they didn't even know. Like they didn't know we had an airfield. They didn't know how much warehouse storage capacity we had. Basically, they didn't know much about our infrastructure—railroads, storage igloos. There were four or five of us—George Windle, Bruce Johnson, Brooke Brewer, two of us union people, myself and John Hennessey—who knew all about the ammunition side of it. We corresponded with the BRAC

Committee at least three to five times a week, giving them updates of our infrastructure. There were certain criteria that we had to meet—like rocket and ammunition maintenance, etc.—that demanded certain facilities. We had it all at our depot basically, very little more would have to be built to meet all the criteria.

When it was all done and said, it was the decision of the BRAC committee that we stay open. But we knew that the political process had overridden any other considerations. Amo Houghton, the congressman whose district included the depot area, had come up a couple times to meet with us but we knew it was just a "dog and pony show"—that either he wasn't interested in us or that he knew that the decision had already been made. Within all that, it was frustrating that the BRAC Committee didn't already know about our capabilities.

The Sierra base in California had the political clout. There was no reason they should have stayed open instead of us, except for one reason. They always received "marginal" at best on their evaluations. The one thing that saved them was that a lot of our ammunition to be demilitarized was sent out there. When you detonated explosives, you were limited as to the total weight you couldn't exceed, so Sierra had an advantage being located in a desert area. At the Seneca Depot, you couldn't exceed one hundred pounds explosive weight per detonation while Sierra could do ten thousand pounds. We here at the Seneca Depot always felt that the Sierra base had a lot more support—political or whatever—than we did.

For the most part, Bruce Johnson, the last civilian head at the Seneca Depot, went out of his way to make sure that people took full advantage of whatever perks were afforded them, such as early retirement. Veterans held an advantage over nonveterans, because they got certain points toward their years of service. When it came down to retention of one position and two people having the same qualifications and one is a veteran, then the veteran had to be retained. There were a few instances where nonveterans were retained, but this was going to happen almost always. There are so many regulations and rules that you can bend and twist or interpret to make the situation look differently than it really is.

The army had arbitrarily decided that it was going to close the base. The military had already gone through one or two rounds of the BRAC process. We thought that it was the lesser of two evils for the depot to undergo the BRAC process rather than have the army arbitrarily end the employment of all the depot workers. The depot was put under the 1995 BRAC.

The $40,000 expense for the lawsuit challenging the army's unilateral decision to close the depot as soon as possible without going through the BRAC process made it possible for employees to take advantage of opportunities under BRAC—for instance, better retirement options and relocation to stay in the federal sector, which gave the community more money under BRAC. The army's plan was just to get rid of five hundred jobs immediately, which would be involuntary separation. We went from around one thousand people who would be affected to less than fifty because of the extra time and being under BRAC. There were probably well over one hundred people—who between the army's initial plans for immediate closure and the depot actually going through the BRAC process—who were able to retire because they got the additional time (a good year and a half). This impacted the local economy because those people didn't have to relocate. The local community really got something back because of its efforts to stop the army from immediately closing the depot.

I was the president of AFGE (American Federation of Government Employees) #2546 in 1994 when Bernard Huff resigned. I got so burned out with all of this that I resigned as head of the union. Probably the biggest reason is that not all of the turmoil and negativity was from the army in that whole process, but when I had employee after employee coming up to my office to beg and plead why they should be on the list to stay (i.e. dependents who have medical issues, or just a few months to go before they can retire). Just the stress from the employees level is what really prompted me to stop. Everything was pretty much in place for the base closure so all that was left to do was to make sure that the procedures that govern retention were adhered to. There were two more union leaders after me: Tony Kominiarek and Bennett Alongi.

Under the BRAC process, if a depot employee was going to transfer to another federal job in another part of the country, the depot employee was entitled to be placed on a list for job opportunities throughout the entire federal sector. If the depot employee took a job at another federal sector, the BRAC process provided that the government would provide the funds for the person to go for a week to the area of that new job and look for housing. If the person's house here in the area of the Seneca

Depot didn't sell within thirty days, then the government would buy the house to resell. The government would also bear the cost of moving the former depot employee. These programs would never have been available to the depot employees without BRAC.

Management and employees were really united during the time period between seeking the injunction and the time we were officially placed on BRAC for closure. That unity ended as soon as we were placed on the BRAC list. I assume management had its procedures to follow from that point—to get the base closed as quickly and as cheaply as possible.

George Windle is the one who turned in the $160,000 that was already appropriated for a new water tower. This is one example of when it was announced that we were for closure, how management "turned." The close working relationship between union and management came to an end once closure was announced. Windle handled the money, so you saw this "turn" more in him than you did in Bruce Johnson. There was never a problem for anyone who had to work outside to get a pair of Carhart coveralls if they needed them to accomplish their work. Once closure was announced, Windle cut out most approvals for almost anything requested. I think it is possible that top management got some kind of financial reward for their expeditious closure that resulted in the saving of a lot of money by the Defense Department than would have otherwise incurred. It is also important to point out that the management at Seneca Depot was so much into a "fast closure" process, while there are yet today bases still open that were on the BRAC list as far back as two closure lists prior to the one that the Seneca Depot had been placed on.

Windle was the head financial guy at the depot in the closure process. He had come to the depot as an active duty military soldier. He worked his way up to ultimately becoming the head financial guy. All in all, he had the respect of virtually all employees. Some of that respect wasn't quite as strong because of his actions during the fast tracking of base closure. Many employees were wondering where his head was at in terms of protecting the local community. Maybe the "army guy" came out in him in the end. Everyone was shocked to learn of his tragic death. There was a plaque in his memory erected in the Seneca Army Depot Employees Credit Union (which later merged with Summit).

The local community didn't really respond by providing support for our efforts to stop the army from closing the depot in the way that I thought they should and would. However, those that did worked tirelessly to support our cause, resulting in a much less negative impact upon the local economy. We had to come up and basically beg the [Seneca] county board of supervisors for a resolution supporting the depot staying open. There were a couple board members who from the very beginning were completely devoted to our cause, because they knew the implications of Depot closure. Jim Garlick of the town of Fayette held many meetings with local politicians and management at the Depot. That is where SOS (Save Our Seneca) started. We were devastated by the article in the Rochester *Democrat and Chronicle* quoting Chick Sinicropi (chairman of the county board of supervisors at the time) saying "Maybe it's time to find another use for the depot." That's when the gloves came off. This angered the workforce. Maybe it was good in that it motivated the workforce to fight the army's plans. We (depot employees and family members—the KOBRA group) had a walk from the county office building to People's Park in downtown Seneca Falls where we met with State Legislator Michael Nozzolio. This was done to bring more attention to what was going on. We were not pleased with the limited support we got from the local community.

We became a Depot Activity under the Toby Hanna Army Depot in Pennsylvania. Not surprisingly, when Toby Hanna got a directive to reduce workforce, the Seneca facility was the first place they looked at to reduce positions.

One of the CEOs at this time really didn't do anything to help us in our efforts to keep the depot in business. We were going to have an added mission to our IPE activities—a new big building was going to be built just south of the existing IPE buildings—but it didn't happen. There was going to be a new firehouse for the North End and a covering for the swimming pool, but it didn't happen under his watch. He didn't go to the conferences where work was divvied out among the various depots, so not surprisingly our depot didn't get anything. Perhaps he knew that our depot wasn't going to get these new missions, so he didn't go. Perhaps he had certain "marching orders" from the army, but perhaps he was not doing his job. The bottom line is that getting new missions and having these kinds of renovations done would perhaps have kept the depot open.

BETTY SERVEN

INTERVIEWED BY NAOMI BREWER

I started work at the depot in 1970, working in the commissary until I got my special weapons clearance. I retired at the end of 1989 and worked in Q, health building A, the garage ordering parts for machinery and did some traveling as ordering officer going to Hartford, Connecticut, off and on for over two years.

I was born in the town of Ovid between Ovid and Lodi. My father had been in service in World War I. After his discharge, he worked for Eastman farms, bought a farm on McCulloch Road. I started school in the little schoolhouse on 414 where Joe Trainor's sister was my first teacher. My dad lost the milk farm when he participated in a milk strike because the dairy farmers weren't making any money. We moved to Sutton Road just above the railroad track in a house owned by Freem Doane. I went to the Sutton School with Mrs. Bailey (Miss Marie Withiam). The people that lived in the big house nearby were the Dean family.

I remember Donald Crane and Malcolm Updike who walked with us to the country school. In the area where they park now along 96A, there used to be a long metal bar that you could tie horses up to. We kids used to play there as we walked to and from school.

As a kid I went to the Kendaia Baptist Church. I remember standing in Children's Day with poison ivy all down my legs, my legs all wrapped up.

My father and mother, Ernest Craig and Grace Artley Craig, worked for the WPA. When the depot bought the property, they moved to just across from where the Sampson Museum is now. When the Sampson Naval Station came in 1942, my family was forced to relocate from this new place. My dad worked for the Coryell fruit farm. Some of those fruit trees are still on Sampson. Their next move was to Route 96A across from the gate nearby the underpass (where Maybees live now).

While we were there, the army was also buying lake property. The Allman sisters didn't want to sell their property. The police came and moved all their furniture out on the lawn. My father and other men loaded up the furniture and got it out of the weather. The sisters moved to a cobblestone house on McGiver Road.

I felt that there were an awful lot of people who felt that the government didn't pay them properly. One of them was a Mr. Thorpe. He was very upset. The Thorpes moved to Geneva. My father was so disappointed about losing his farm that he never owned another farm. I had five brothers and five sisters, so he had to find work someplace just to feed us. When my older brother went into the service, my dad went to work at Sampson in the boiler room.

There were a lot of houses on the government property that the people had moved. Mildred and Dick Voight moved their house from Baptist Church Road next to the old Varick firehouse on East Lake Road. Some of the houses on depot lake property were moved there from the depot. One had belonged to Montford. My job was to oversee all the kitchen appliances, etc. put into these homes on East Lake Road.

I best remember supervisor Jim O'Connell. We pulled a trick on him once. We all went together and bought lottery tickets. Somehow or other he told us that we had won, and the whole office was celebrating. Then he told us he was just kidding. So the next day we got back at him by taking the ink in the copy machine and opening up his telephone and put it in the talking and hearing parts. He had black all over his face. Later his wife, Joy, told me that she had been wondering how he got so dirty that day.

Most of my new jobs were promotions. It was in IPE that I did the traveling. I worked with Pat Jones who was secretary in Q area. She knew June Kearns, who was the secretary to the commander. Some of the depot ladies still get together once a month and go to lunch.

I enjoyed working in the Q area, although it was stressful at times. Sometimes we had to cross over the road to check out things in maintenance area. If the MPs were in the midst of an exercise, there could be big security problems.

When I was working in the housing area, Mrs. Jarmond called the night before Thanksgiving. She had her turkey in the stove, and it stopped cooking, 12:30 at night. I had to go in and open up my warehouse and get another stove and take it down to Mrs. Jarmond's house. She normally in daytime had a driver and truck at her beck and call. This time she got the man at the gate and a friend and their truck to use to get the new stove.

Regarding the Women's Peace Encampment—that got to be quite an ordeal. It made it very difficult for workers to get into work. One morning we couldn't get in at the Hillside gate or the next one south. When we got to the gate across from Sampson, we saw a man motioning for us to go in that gate. We went in that gate and then had to drive all around to get to our work. The women protesters then blocked that gate as well. Some workers couldn't get into work that day. Everybody was annoyed with what they were doing.

My daughter, Gail, remembers that at my retirement party Colonel Timmons said my job had a worldwide effect on Army operations.

John Stahl

Interviewed by Walter Gable and Naomi Brewer

I started work at the depot in 1943. I was being paid sixty-seven and a half cents an hour. I was seventeen when I graduated from high school and was hired as a munitions handler, but I couldn't go to work until age eighteen (about three–four weeks later). I had an asthma problem so I couldn't keep up work as a munitions handler. They needed someone to gas and spot lift trucks and generators, so I used a truck to do this. After a while, I became a lift truck operator.

As a forklift truck operator, I got dispatched to an igloo where we were handling boxes marked "Manhattan Project." Me and my fellow workers were wondering at the time why there was something that belonged in Manhattan being stored at the depot. I got dispatched to the LCL (Less than Carload Lots) where I operated a tractor-trailer and a lift truck. There was one boxcar there—they opened the car and the only thing in that car was a drum in the corner—packed in anti-freeze. There were specific instructions how that drum was to be handled. When the drum was out on the platform, all the "big wheels" had to come down from the office to see that drum. The drum was put on my trailer and put in a little igloo down in A area. There were two small igloos down there. I couldn't take the drum down to that igloo until I had a guard escort. The "wheels" followed us down to make sure the drum was handled in a certain way. When the news reported about the Manhattan Project, my fellow workers and I could put together what that drum was.

I got involved with a few things I didn't like. One day I was called into the colonel's office, expecting to be reprimanded for doing something wrong. Instead, the colonel told me that I was going to do a very special new project. At the time we had a missile base in Germany, and the shelf life of those missiles there was winding down to the point they were to be replaced with new missiles. As these were nuclear missiles that would have to go through the Berlin Corridor to get to their intended bases in Germany, the Russians needed to know all the specific facts about them, so that the exchanged missiles were going to be the same in terms of range and destructive capability. I oversaw the loading of the replacement missiles on the plane at the depot that was then going to Germany. I knew every move that that aircraft made. I had continuous messages about its status. "Oh, by the way, one mistake could start World War Three," the colonel told me when I was first being told by the colonel about this project.

Then I got involved in the Cuban Missile Crisis. About four of us knew where the missiles were. One of us four was on call twenty-four–seven. We had a good idea when the missiles were moved into Cuba and where they could be targeted to hit in the United States. I knew where plans (for U.S. missile retaliation or strike) were located on the depot so that I could go get them if necessary. It was part of the job; that's what I did. You got used to it.

AEC was going to leave, and the army was already leaving and the South End was going to take over. I didn't like what the South End was doing. So there was an opening in inventory, and I put in for that job. While at inventory, the depot took over the airfield. I worked at the airfield for a couple years—made shipments all over. So I also had an air force clearance.

While I was working at the air strip, during one air strike, some Ovid area woman, who was in the air force and home on leave, came up to the girl in the office and told this office worker that she had to be at a base in California at a certain date. The girl in the office was trying to make arrangements for this woman to get on some commercial flight to California so that she could then get to Japan. This was happening at a time when the commercial airline was on strike. The girl in the office asked me if there was something I could do to help get this woman to California. So I helped get her on a flight out of the depot airstrip, a flight that had brought in materials from Texas and was returning to Texas. The man in Texas held another flight for two hours so that she could make the connection from Texas to California. He didn't know who that girl was and he would like to find out what happened. The following Monday morning, he got a message: "Package delivered on time."

When the airstrip job was made permanent, I couldn't qualify. So I wound up in data processing. The depot wanted to get rid of everyone with more than twenty-five years, so I retired. When I retired in 1972 (after twenty-nine years), I had to sign a document that I would not discuss North Depot Activity for seven years.

There wasn't many things I missed while working here.

One decision I had to make down at the demo pit where unstable explosives were destroyed was what to do when a plane was in the air at the time we were planning to detonate the last blast of the day. The hole filled with explosives couldn't be left over night, but it couldn't be detonated with the plane approaching. So I decided to fire off one blast, and that plane (probably down by Interlaken) immediately changed its course significantly. We all laughed at how we had scared that plane away!

As for the Italian POWs, I thought it was a peaceful situation. They were happy to be here—three square meals a day, they were pretty much limited to go only where the depot security told them they could go. They didn't want to go back to fight war. They had their own barracks. They did odd jobs. We weren't around them too much. They worked in a group up on combat (the warehouses were called that). Some of the workers who worked up there were very uptight about these Italian POWs because some of them had been fighting the Italians down in North Africa.

The Popping Plant was a unique building. It broke down thirty- and fifty-caliber ammo and had the furnace. When you fed the furnaces, you had to be careful not to feed it too fast or the fire would come up out of the furnaces like you wouldn't believe!

I remember seeing the first white deer. A group of workers were going down to standard magazines one morning. The guys on the back of the truck saw a white deer. We heard all kinds of stories. The white deer were there long before the NDA. One guy found a carcass and took measurements—that guy thought it was a strain from upper Canada. They thought the deer had been dropped off at the depot because the deer stayed in this one area off Route 96A. I speculated that a hunting group from Waterloo that often went up to Alaska may well have stunned a white deer up there and then brought it to be released at the depot, as some kind of practical joke. Those deer would go over the fence like it wasn't even there. We would work in the igloos, and they would be right across. We got along with them, and they got along with us.

Respect explosives, don't fear them. That was the best piece of advice ever given to me by a person working at the depot.

At the airfield, I remember that the first jet came in on a Sunday. I had a good tour of the jet and wondered if the strip was long enough for the jet to take off. They found it was. On takeoff the jet was only about halfway down the airstrip when the pilot raised the jet up into the air. "The pilot called back on the radio and asked, 'Do you think your strip is long enough?'" Obviously it was more than "long enough."

If there was to be a night shipment out of the Q area, I had to talk with the sergeant who would be on duty that night. In that talk, which took place in the afternoon, I would have to tell him who all would be coming in with me. For some shipments that went out of Q area, an electrician would have to open up the electric fence.

I had the plans for the airstrip. These plans showed that this airstrip was built from the beginning to accommodate jets, and nobody seemed to know that. North Star had some kind of an arrangement with the depot. They would fly in and out using the airstrip. When I had anything coming in at the airstrip, they, however, had to leave. Besides the air force, AEC flew in and out. They would come in, offload and then fly to Syracuse and refuel. The next day, they would come back to the depot.

On another occasion, after AEC was no longer at the depot, sometime after a flight had left the depot as part of the regular shipments from the depot, I got a phone call from the aircraft commander. He told me the plane was out over the ocean and had been struck by lightning. The pilot was coming back to the depot airstrip because he didn't know if there was any damage to the items he was carrying. The items were removed from the plane and taken elsewhere in the depot for inspection. New replacement items were put on the plane, and the pilot left. This incident also helps to illustrate that much of my work involved things happening off the depot premises—shipping overseas, for instance. You had different things to think about. I think the items on that plane were in all probability nuclear weapons.

At the popping plant, they had two big furnaces. In the other room, they had four big machines that would cut the cartridge case of the shell and then take out the powder. The chute had a vacuum hooked to it that took the powder out to a building some distance away. The only fire safety procedure was a whistle. I warned them several times that this whistle was inadequate. The tracer dust was a constant problem. One night, there was a fire and the sprinkler system didn't activate. Two of us—the boss and myself—went back in even though it was a violation of procedures. The boss pulled the hand sprinkler. I went out into the powder collection unit and told the guy to stop the vacuum unit. Both of us got called down by our bosses for going back into that building. We did it because the man out in the powder collection room was unaware of the fire. After this incident, they put in a siren horn system in both places.

One of the things I laugh about today is when I was an inspector. The women couldn't wear nylons or anything that made a spark when they were working in black powder. So the government issued different color underwear for each day. As the inspector, I had to make sure the women were wearing the right underwear.

While I was working in inventory (after I had left NDA), I was told by my current boss to pick up a sedan and go to the Q area. I didn't know why I was to do this until I got there and was told that the NDA people had flunked their IG inspection twice and that their entire mission was in jeopardy because of this. When I was there, there had never been any trouble with inspections. I was handed the IG reports, and I followed up on what the IG had caught. I found a way to straighten out these things. I wrote down everything that could be done to correct what the IG had found. I also wrote down what I found. When we had the critique, believe me, I had some unhappy people. One worker said that he thought he and I were friends, but the critique was unfavorable of him. I reassured him that we were friends, that my report contained no names, but that these bad things had to be changed to pass future IG inspections.

Because there was an "eye in the sky" (i.e., spy satellites), there were two major ways in which we tried to prevent spying from taking place. There were some things we transported on trucks that we covered up so the "eye in the sky" couldn't tell what we had on the trucks. Also, there were metal boxes put on the entrances to the igloos so that the "eye in the sky" couldn't look into the open door entrance to these igloos and see what was inside.

To enter a structure, you had to have a jack phone and call in the code of the day. Every day the code changed. One experience I had was in the middle of the night. It was about 11:30 that I opened a warehouse, went in and got the stuff I needed for the shipment. Then I came out and secured the warehouse and made the shipment. I came back and opened the warehouse. The time now was about 12:30. I called in and gave them the code, went in the warehouse and came out. When I came out there were spotlights on me and guns on me. I asked, 'What's going on?' They told me that I had given the wrong code. Then I talked them into letting me talk to the operator on the other end. What I did was say that I had given the right code. I said, "Look at your clock and look at the code for that date." After the operator found out that I had given the right code, the operator asked to have one of the guards put on the jack phone. The guard listened on the jack phone, and the incident was over. The codes every day were simple. For example, the code for the day might be "20." The operator would say "10," and then I would say "10 and 10 makes 20."

Not many people knew about the Disassembly Plant. It was a big concrete barricade with a rod that went through it. On one side the rod was connected to an electric motor. On the other side of this concrete barricade, the shell would be mounted in a vice so that the pin wrench would go into the BD fuse. The forklift truck would bring in a six-inch shell that would be put in the vice because they were heavy. Once this was completed, we would go into the shed and start the motor, which would unscrew the fuse. There was a TV camera focused on it. The fuse would be taken out, and then the rounds were taken down to the demo pit so that the explosives could be burned out. The metal would then be salvaged.

Phil Stannard

Interviewed by Allan Buddle

I began work at the depot in July 1968 and was paid $2.20 per hour. Shortly afterward, during the Vietnam War, I enlisted in the air force and was sent to San Antonio, Texas, for basic training. While there, I sunburned my eyes and eventually received a medical discharge. Returning to Interlaken, I asked for a job at the depot back but was told they had no openings. I contacted Assemblyman Lee and Congressman Horton, and very soon afterward I got a call from the depot asking me to come back to work.

One of my first jobs was packing guns for shipment to Viet Nam. They painted the corners of the boxes yellow to indicate that their destination was Viet Nam. I also still remember how cold I got loading trailers containing compressors and generators onto railroad cars for shipment. We were required to wear steel-toed shoes, and my feet were just frozen all the time. The only place to warm up was in a bathroom in one of the warehouses, and you needed permission to go there. My job was to crawl under the trailers on the decks of the railroad cars and, using No. 9 wire, fasten the trailers to the cars. After the wires were fastened then sticks had to be used to twist the wires tight and then the sticks had to be wired down so they wouldn't loosen during shipment. The safety inspector would come by once in a while and stomp on your toe. If you weren't wearing your steel-toed shoes, you were sent home without pay.

In the early years of my employment at the depot, I and many others reported in the morning to a central place and were given an assignment for the day. We never knew whether we would be inside or out, so didn't know how to dress.

In 1975, I became a Motor Vehicle Operator in the Mail Room. I and another person went to the Romulus Post Office each day and picked up the mail for the entire depot. For this job, I had a high-level security clearance. The mail was separated into deliveries for the Military Police and for the Headquarters Companies (Special Weapons). Each military unit had their own mail clerk. I took the mail to the Companies and to the Q Area. Confidential messages came in by teletype. I signed for them and delivered them to the classified documents office. A clerk would determine who they were for, and I would deliver them and get a signature that the documents had been delivered to the right person.

When you went to the Q Area, they took your badge, gave you another and did a complete inspection of your vehicle. The reverse happened on the way out of the Q Area. If you didn't have the appropriate security clearance, an MP rode with you with his gun trained on you.

I remember a couple of instances where volunteers were asked to come in on a Saturday, go to the Q Area, form a line and drive the deer out of the area through a gate that was opened just for that purpose. Snow fence was set up to keep the deer from getting in between the three rows of fences at the open gate.

During the Peace Encampment days, Jim McLaughlin was supervisor and I was leader. I didn't like it when Jim was off because he was responsible for the twenty-eight people in the unit in three different locations. The army brought in reinforcements during the Peace Encampment. There would be huge planeloads of Jeeps delivered to the airstrip. The planes had three decks with ramps that could be lowered for the Jeeps to drive down. I could not believe the number of Jeeps that were on each one of the planes. I worked a lot of overtime during the Peace Encampment period as well as during Desert Storm. When on overtime while working for Roads and Grounds, you were allowed to eat in the Mess Hall.

One Saturday, I and seven others sat all day in a van on the airstrip waiting for a plane that was coming for a load of cots being sent to the Philippines following a hurricane there. The plane finally landed, and it barely cleared the roof of the van, rocking it and practically tipping it over. The cots were all loaded on trailers ready to be loaded onto the plane.

While supervisor in Jim McLaughlin's absence, I would sometimes spend all day on paperwork. Each person was required to keep a time sheet with codes for each activity performed during the day and the amount of time spent on each activity. All of that data had to be entered into a computer the next day. To get to my office, I had to go through three padlocked doors and had to be last out at night and be sure that all the lights were turned off and all the doors locked.

A siren would blow at the end of the day, and that would trigger a stampede of workers getting to their cars so they could get out of the gate. However the warehouses were at the south end of the depot and the administrative area was at the north end, so all of those employees' cars were in line first. Randomly the MPs would check cars on the way out, and when that was observed, some cars would pull out of line, turn around and go back, probably to dump whatever they had that was not supposed to be taken from the depot.

When the RIF was announced, I had worked at the depot for twenty-four years and eight months and needed twenty-five years to retire. Fortunately for me, enough people took the retirement incentive that I was transferred to Shipping and able to continue working until March 1995, when I had twenty-seven years and ten months with accumulated sick leave.

FLORENCE VARGASON

INTERVIEWED BY NAOMI BREWER

My parents, Charles W. Lisk and Elenora (Worden) Lisk, lived on a farm two miles down the road [west] from the Mt. Green Cemetery in Romulus, New York. Charles was a schoolteacher, but when his father died he had to take over the farm. It was a crop farm, and he also had cattle—horses, cows and chickens.

I was the youngest of their four children. When I was nine years old, my mother died, so my father brought me up. I went to the Ludlum country school, which was one mile on down the road from our home. I went there through the seventh grade, then a bus took me to the Romulus School. Across the road from the Ludlum School was a Methodist church. And in that area was the big farm of John Lisk (brother to Charles). John had a wife and children and a hired man. He farmed and raised chickens and sold them. This farm was also taken by the government for the Seneca Army Depot, also, the church and school.

By 1940, my older siblings had left home. That same year, I married Charley Vargason, and we two moved in with his parents, Art and Maggie Vargason, on their farm east of Ovid.

It was in 1941 that the government ordered my father to leave his farm, as it was on the site of the soon-to-be Seneca Ordnance Depot. He sold his cattle and began moving his possessions to live with me and my family. He and I went back the second day of his moving to get the rest of things and found that all was gone—stolen. Dad had lost a beautiful hanging lamp plus other items. Dad was more upset when he found that all of his crop of cucumbers had been stolen from his garden.

ERNIE WALDEN

INTERVIEWED BY ALLAN BUDDLE

My dad, Carl, had worked at the depot in the 1940s. He had been driving trucks for the Swift Meat Co. of Ithaca, even making deliveries to some of the CCC camps. The company decided to move operations to Elmira, and Carl choose to work at the depot instead of moving. Dad drove semi trucks and later dump trucks until he retired from the depot.

I began at the Seneca Army Depot in 1953. During the course of my employment there, I held a number of different positions. I finally left in 1970 to take a job at Willard.

Initially I worked in the small arms group, sealing cans of fifty-caliber machine gun bullets. The women packed the cans, sent them down the line and I sealed them.

My work on the demolition grounds was hard work but fun. This involved blowing up ammunition that was not up to standards. The boxes of "bad ammo" arrived in trucks, cushioned inside the trucks with sand bags. The demolition grounds had a series of large holes, about the size of small rooms. The men would go down into the hole holding the boxes of ammunition. Ernie mentioned rifle grenades. It was not advisable to tip the boxes. They should be held upright. The boxes were carefully placed, and dirt was shoveled over the hole by hand. All the holes were wired to a dugout, an underground concrete shelter. When all the ammunition was placed in the holes and covered with dirt, the men retreated to the dugout. When all were safely in place, one hole at a time was ignited.

As the work force was reduced, I became a grounds person, mowing grass. I then spent ten years in insect/rodent control. I sprayed for cockroaches in the houses and offices, as well as for mosquitoes along the lake. Woodchucks were a problem in that they could eat through the water-proofing seal on the igloos under the grass. I trapped or shot the woodchucks. In addition, I applied herbicides around the perimeter fence.

For a period of time, I worked in the warehouse. The next position was in salvage. I spent a good bit of time helping to facilitate sales of old machinery—not exactly my job but appreciated by my supervisor.

My last position was in the commissary. When my hours of employment were to be changed, I finally decided—enough. I left the Seneca Army Depot for good in 1970.

Glenn White

Interviewed by Carolyn Zogg

I was hired August 16, 1951, as an ammunition handler, a civil service job, with starting salary of $1.19 per hour. My major duties were physically moving ammunition, ammunition components and explosive items during storage and/or transportation. I soon found out physically moving ammunition was hard work. On December 19, 1951, I was accepted as a forklift operator with a salary of $1.25 per hour. The duties consisted of operating all types of forklifts (combustible engine and/or battery, depending on work location). I worked in General Supply and Ammunition Area as directed.

On March 19 of 1952, I was drafted in the marine corp and released on March 9, 1954.

On March 15, 1954, I returned to work at the Seneca Army Depot and was reinstated as a forklift operator with the salary of $1.64 per hour. I couldn't believe the salary increase after being away for two years. I was accepted as a Surveillance Inspector August 23 the same year, with the same pay grade and salary. Then I was accepted to attend the Ammunition Inspector School at Savanna Army Depot, Savanna, Illinois. On completion of the training, I returned to the Seneca Army Depot June 20, 1955 as an Ammunition Inspector trainee, promoted to GS-5 with a salary of $3,940 per annum. When I completed trainee status, I was promoted to Ammunition Inspector, GS-6, salary $4,215 per year. During the time working at the Seneca Army Depot as an Ammunition Inspector, my goal was to work my way through the ranks to become the Chief of Surveillance. This was a GS-13 position.

On January 13, 1958, I was transferred to Letterkenny Army Depot with a promotion to GS-7 and with the same duties. After my tour at Letterkenny, I was moved to Korea, Western Military Transportation command, Oakland California; Red River Army Depot, Vietnam; US Army Defense Ammunition Center and School; Eighth Logistic Command, Italy, US Army Southern European Task Force, Italy; Savanna Army Depot; US Army Support Command, Hawaii; U.S. Army Defense Ammunition Center and School again, and again to Korea in 1987.

On my return from Korea, I was assigned back home to the Seneca Army Depot as Director of Quality Assurance, formerly Chief Ammunition Inspector. I retired August 4, 1988. My working goal was attained.

As a young teenager, maybe twelve or thirteen, I remember going to the local Friday Night Square Dance at the Lodi Town Hall on Main Street with my friends Leroy Swick, John Carmel, William and Walter Roach. It was the only entertainment in town in 1943, and it didn't cost us anything to check out the familiar crowd dancing to the music of Charlie Stahl's Dancing Band on the second floor. There was a six to one ratio of women to men—the men were the Italian prisoners of war bussed up from the Seneca Army Depot where they were being detained during the war. About twenty, uniformly dressed in olive drab shirts and trousers, arrived by bus accompanied by two armed guards. The guards were then stationed at the front and back doors of the Town Hall to make sure no prisoner left the building. Not that a prisoner wanted to. They were having too good a time as dance partners with an overabundance of good-looking women. Curiously enough, these dances were not considered disloyal but just an evening of fun and entertainment for Lodinians.

At intermission, we strolled half a block south to Mildred Steven's Ice Cream Parlor for a bit of refreshment. The attending non-coms and brass continued farther down the block to the Eagle Hotel for a local fish dinner—trout fresh from Seneca Lake, gill netted by Bill Putnam and Jim Baker. And something wet for their thirst. I knew the old saying, "One didn't need a license below the railroad." And as there was no drinking at the town hall, the Eagle Hotel also carried the reputation of the "Unofficial Officer's Club Extended." Feeling good with food and drink, the men would then descend to the hotel basement for a game of cards, usually not returning to the dance.

In the 1970s when me and my family were stationed in Italy after the war, one of my employees, a former Italian prisoner of war detained in Europe, decried the fact that he wasn't one of the "fortunate" ones who had been held in the United States, with its good food and entertainment.

I saw my first white deer on the depot in the fall of 1955. The winter of 1955 was one of the worst in many years. There was deep snow from November until the spring of 1956, and major winterkill of the deer herd was noted. It was estimated many hundreds of deer died. Photographs from the air showed bodies of deer covered with snow, looking like moguls on a ski slope.

Several attempts were made to control the size of the herd in 1956. None proved to be economically feasible, so it was determined to have a controlled hunt. The Commander of the Depot had authority over the first hunt.

The first controlled hunt was conducted in 1956 with assistance from the NYS Department of Conservation and Cornell University. All harvested (killed) deer were properly tagged with NYS hunting documentation, and each carcass was examined for health defects prior to being released from the depot. Many tissue samples were collected by biologists for research to ascertain the health of the herd.

The second controlled hunt was conducted in the fall of 1957. The same procedures as previously in 1956 were followed.

When I was transferred to Letterkenny Army Depot in January 1957, Letterkenny experienced the same problem with deer herd management and resorted to controlled hunts. These hunts are still in effect today. With proper management, viable deer herds can be sustained in closed, fenced environment. There were deer herds at Red River, Texas; Savanna, Illinois; and Sierra Army Depot, California, but none had the white deer that the Seneca Army Depot had.

Robert Zemanek Jr.

Interviewed by Walter Gable

I went to work at the Seneca Ordnance Depot with the security police force in February 1972, after having been in the army. In December 1972, I became the Information (Public Affairs) Officer. I retired in 1990.

Regarding the logo that is used by the Seneca Depot, it came out of a contest. Colonel Alden Cox wanted a patch that would incorporate the white deer, and a Pennsylvania company came up with a patch that looked just terrible. So, there was this design contest. [The winning design came from Pat Matriceno, Judith Connolly and Gary Smith, according to the article in the October 31, 1979 issue of the *Depot Dispatch*.] This logo was used on everything, but it was never officially adopted by the Department of Defense.

There was a *Seneca Drums* paper that was run off on mimeo. It contained an article that the Seneca Depot played a role in the Manhattan Project, handling one thousand barrels of crude uranium ore from the Belgian Congo that came to the Seneca Depot from New Jersey. This material was placed in the last row of "E" block of igloos—the ammo area. In the 1970s, I was contacted by FUSRAP program of the Department of Energy. I went out with those people when they examined and tested this storage area. They found residual contamination.

It was rather easy to find out if nuclear weapons actually were at the Seneca Depot. For these reasons: (1) the issue of nuclear weapons at this depot was labeled "confidential," which is a very low level of security for the DOD. (2) Certain facts were commonly reported—this depot had more than one hundred nuclear weapons technicians, there was a whole unit of maintenance technicians and the phrase "nuclear weapons installation" was used. (3) There was a major exercise in 1990 to which the media were invited. It was a nuclear weapons accident training exercise.

During the 1983 anti-nuclear weapons demonstrations, I was in daily contact with the women of the Women's Encampment for a Future of Peace and Justice. A few of the women were reasonable, but the majority weren't. It was almost impossible to have rational discussion. People should read *Nuclear Summer* (Louise Krasniewicz author, published by Cornell University Press in 1992), which is an anthropologist's study of how the women acted in this group effort. Twelve thousand women came that summer to demonstrate. No depot people (other than myself) were made available to talk to the media that year. I told the media that depot workers were told they couldn't talk to the media on "government time," but the workers were not told that they could not talk to the media. My basic response to the media was, "People have a right to protest, but this is a political matter. If people have issue with weapons, they should take it up with their congressman. We neither confirm nor deny the existence of nuclear weapons at this facility." This last sentence was the standard response that the DOD gave regarding whether there were nuclear weapons at this facility. I never cleared my responses with the depot commander, but I must have done OK that summer. I was given a special medal for what I did that summer of the protests. It cost $2 million for the depot to deal with what these protesters did that summer.

Some other protesters besides those of the Women's Encampment were Bella Abzug, one of the Berrigan brothers and Dr. Benjamin Spock. On the day that Spock would ultimately get arrested, I can tell this interesting story. One of my assistants told me that some woman wanted to talk with me as soon as possible. I went to meet her and this lady approached me and identified herself as Dr. Spock's wife. She said that her husband was too old to climb over the fence to commit his act of civil disobedience and that she was asking that the fence be opened up, or something else done, so that he wouldn't have to climb over the fence to commit his act of civil disobedience. I said that no special accommodations were going to be made. So, what actually happened was that people helped Dr. Spock to climb over the fence.

I am proud that there was not even one single instance of reported mistreatment coming out of all those protests that year. I was only forty in 1983. I felt that my work that year of protests was the highlight of my professional career.

Eleven other depots besides the Seneca Depot were part of a general authorization for early retirements in 1990. So, I took it.

The special weapons mission went away in the early 1990s. So the MPs were no longer needed, and the headquarters company went away. It became hard to justify the base's existence to Washington, so there were directives to cut back on the size of the workforce. Five hundred were let go in 1993.

That base [Sierra Army Base at Herlong, California] is still there. It wasn't politics; it was the way that base handled requests for reducing spending, etc. That Sierra base simply wouldn't agree to reductions.

APPENDIX II
BASIC FACT SHEET

Key People and Businesses Involved in the Construction Project

- William S. Lozier, Inc., of Rochester, NY, was the architect-engineer.
- Poirier, McLane and John W. Harris Company of New York City was the general contractor.
- Colonel Paul B. Parker was the Army person in charge of the construction project.
- L.P. Walker of the Real Estate Division of the War Department was in charge of the acquisition of the necessary lands for the project and the removal of those people living on this land.

Key Dates in Seneca Army Depot History

- March 31 and April 1, 1941—Representatives of the War Department made an on-site visit to the mid-Seneca County site.
- June 11, 1941—U.S. Government's War Department announced official approval of $8 million to start a munitions project in Central New York state.
- July 9, 1941—Construction of the Seneca Ordnance Depot began with initial target date of May 1, 1942, for completion of the construction project.

- August 9, 1941—War Department General Order No. 8 established the Seneca Ordnance Depot.
- September 15, 1941—The Ordnance Corps officially took over the operation of the Seneca Ordnance Depot, with Captain J.L. Clark in command.
- November 15, 1941—The last of the five hundred munitions igloos were completed.
- January 6, 1942—The first incoming shipment of ammunition was received at the depot.
- January 31, 1942—The first outgoing shipment of ammunition from the depot was made.
- July 16, 1942—Construction began on additional warehouses (for storage of general supply items) and miscellaneous buildings.
- November 30, 1942—The Combat Equipment Storage Area (later known as the General Supply Storage Area) received its first shipment of general supplies.
- February 2, 1955—At the north end of the depot, 1,120 acres were transferred to the New York District of the Corps of Engineers for the construction of additional buildings for "a new storage activity" (later referred to as "special weapons").
- October 2, 1956—The above site was established as the North Storage Activity (Class II Activity).
- Spring 1956—The first white fawn was seen on the depot property.
- November 14, 1958—The former Sampson Air Force Base airstrip and facilities and certain other buildings (including 21 family housing units along Seneca Lake) were turned over to the depot.
- October 19, 1959—A contract was awarded for the construction of the 120-family unit Capehart Housing facilities.
- March 31, 1960—Depot chapel is dedicated.
- September 7, 1961—The North Depot Activity was consolidated with the Seneca Ordnance Depot, effective January 1, 1962.
- August 1, 1962—Seneca Ordnance Depot facility was transferred from the Chief of Ordnance to the U.S. Army Supply and Maintenance Command, and the facility was renamed the Seneca Army Depot (SEAD).

- July 1, 1966—Seneca Army Depot was reassigned to the U.S. Army Materiel Command.
- Aug 2, 1978—LORAN-C Transmitting Station dedicated (a U.S. Coast Guard facility located on a portion of the Depot property, a facility used by ships and aircraft as far away as 1000 miles to guide them in their flight and navigation).
- July 28, 1983—Women's Peace Encampment sets up its residence on a farm just north of the village of Romulus to use as a home site for demonstrations throughout that summer against the deployment of Pershing II and Cruise missiles (nuclear weapons at the Depot).
- Oct 1995—Seneca Army Depot approved for the Base Realignment and Closure (BRAC) list; final base closure came in 2000.[243]
- July 2000—KidsPeace National Center of NY, Inc., Seneca Wood campus, opened in the northern end of former depot property.
- Summer 2000—Five Points Correctional Facility opened at extreme southeast end of former depot property.
- Sept 30, 2003—About 7,000 acres of the former depot was transferred to Seneca County with the intent being that the Seneca County Industrial Development Agency will continue to seek uses of this former depot property for the economic viability of the county.

Changes in Name of This Facility

- 1941—Seneca Ordnance Depot
- 1962—Seneca Army Depot (SEAD)

APPENDIX III
COMMANDING OFFICERS AT THE SENECA DEPOT[244]

Year Began	Name
1941	Captain J.L. Clark
1942	Colonel Joseph G. Smith
1943	Colonel Arthur D. Elliot
1948	Lieutenant Colonel Robert L. Judson
1950	Colonel J. Paul Lawther
1951	Lieutenant Colonel John B. Deane
1952	Colonel Thomas W. Cooke
1954	Colonel Walter F. Partin
1956	Colonel Charles L. Simpson
1956	Colonel Franklin Kemble, Jr.
1960	Colonel William L. Clay
1962	Colonel John S. Chambers, Jr.
1963	Colonel James O. Green
1965	Colonel William G. Senior
1967	Colonel Howard C. Metzler
1968	Lieutenant Colonel William F. Spicher
1969	Colonel Milton G. Branham

Year Began	Name
1971	Lieutenant Colonel Harry W. Johnson
1971	Colonel Thomas A. Mort
1973	Colonel Allen H. Light Jr.
1975	Colonel Alan A. Nord
1975	Colonel Alden L. Cox
1978	Colonel Fred Hissong, Jr.
1980	Colonel Robert J. Hudak
1982	Colonel John S. Wilson
1985	Colonel Bruce M. Garnett
1987	Colonel William R. Holmes
1989	Colonel Franklin H. Cochran
1991	Colonel James B. Cross
1993	Lieutenant Colonel Roy E. Johnson
1995	Lieutenant Colonel Stephen W. Brooks
1997	Lieutenant Colonel Donald C. Olson
1999	Lieutenant Colonel Brian K. Frank

APPENDIX IV
LIST OF PROPERTY OWNERS DISPOSSESSED IN 1941

Town of Romulus

Parcel Number	Name of Property Owner
88	Baldridge, Charles J.
89	Gates, Wilbur Leroy ET UX
90	Williams, Isaac W.
91	Gates, Clarence E.
92	Gates, Benjamin Franklin ET UX
92A	Covert, Albert J. ET AL
93	Ernsberger, Clayton H. ET UX
94	Baldridge, Charles J.
95	Smith, Winifred A.
96	Litchfield, Julia E.
97	Moses, Leonard D. ET UX
98	Williams, Anna C.
101	Crane, Marion E. ET UX
101A	Osford, Jennie E.

Parcel Number	Name of Property Owner
102	Russell, Lloyd J. ET UX
103	Voigt, Richard ET UX
104	Williams, Harry J.
104A	Sheridan, Robert E. ET UX
105	Bolles, Emma S. ET AL
107	Pontius, Fannie Louise
108	Baldridge, Minnie J. ET AL
108A	Williams, Frank S.
109A	Bogardus, Earl ET UX
109B	Bogardus, Thomas J.
111	Burrett, Horaito
111B	Burrett, Homer A. ET UX
112	Bogardus, Earl ET AL
114	Seneca Falls Savings Bank, The
115	Rundell, Clare M. ET AL
116	Cole, Claudius C. ET AL
117	Cole, Clement B. ET AL
118	First Baptist Cemetery Assoc & Society of Romulus, Trustees of
119	Smith, Winifred A.
120	First Baptish Church of Romulus, NY
121	Howerth, Walter ET UX
121A	Coryell, J. Wallace
123	Kaufman, Charles E. ET AL
124	Jurewicz, Stella
124A	Carey, Anna L.
124B	Troutman, John ET AL
124C	Carey, Anna L.
125	Reeder, Warren
128	Budman, Doc. E.
129	Budman, Doc. E.
130	Garnett, Eileen A.

Parcel Number	Name of Property Owner
132	Kokot, Thomas ET UX
134	Baldridge, Charles J.
135	County of Seneca
136	Baldridge, Mary B.
138	Kirkmire, George F. ET UX
139	Secor, Maude E.
140	Van Fleet, Edward A. ET UX
140A	Trainer, John B. ET UX
104B	Hinman, Frances C. ET UX
104D	Trustees of School District No. 7 of Romulus
141	Carson, Charles C. ET UX
142	Freligh, Cora ET AL
143	Williams, Frank S.
143A	Sturges, Ella
143B	Marsha, Frank A.
145	Brown-Agnast, Daniel W.-Stockholders of The Romulus National Bank
146	Sturges, Thomas ET AL
146A	Godley, Leon B. ET UX
147	O'Conner, Emreson G.—Commissioner Public Welfare Seneca Co.
148	Finger (Tinger ?), Clifford A.ET UX
149	Secor, John G.
151	McGinnis, John ET AL
152	Crane, Vance ET UX
153	Conkling, Albert L. ET UX
153A	Carl, Peter M.
153B	Lehigh Valley Railroad Co.
154	Brace, Joseph
155	Sutton, John M.
158	McElroy, Joseph M. ET AL
158A	Coryell, M. Alice ET AL

Parcel Number	Name of Property Owner
159	Fitzgerald, Margaret
161	Wells, Raymond B.
162	National Bank of Ovid
163	Mahar, Veronica, individually and Ex. Of estate of John Mahar
164	Crane, Vance ET UX
165	Doane, Roy ET UX
165A	Brown-Agnast, Daniel W.-Stockholders of The Romulus National Bank
165B	Carmer, Walter S. ET UX
166	Rooney, Peter ET UX
167	McGinnis, John ET AL
168A	McGinnis, John ET UX
170	Covert, Jessie ET UX
171	Johnson, Daniel A.
171A	Lehigh Valley Railroad Co.
172	Youngberg, Erick Alexander ET UX
173	Doane, Roy ET UX
173A	Quins, Harry
178	O'Conner, Emerson G.—Commissioner Public Welfare Seneca Co.
178A	Troutman, Mort ET AL
179	Yakely, Almoron ET UX
179A	Gleason, David
179B	Cramer, Walter
179C	Lehigh Valley Railroad Co.
180	Freliegn, Clarence N.
181	Cramer, Walter ET UX
182	Dunlap, Charles
183	Blaine, Willis W.
184	Harington, Mary C.
185	Rooney, Peter ET AL

PARCEL NUMBER	NAME OF PROPERTY OWNER
186	Keanie, Paul P.
187	Lehigh Valley Railroad Co.
188	Lehigh Valley Railroad Co.
189	Lehigh Valley Railroad Co.
WL1	Alleman, Elizabeth ET AL
WL2	McWhorter, Archie ET AL
WL3	Smith, Percie B. ET AL
WL4	Hamilton, Anna
WL5	Hagerty, R. Augustus
WL6	Crane, Maurice M.
WL7	Marquart, Leslie A. ET AL
TOWN OF VARICK	
A	General Services Administration
12	Post, Monroe J. ET UX
14	Dwire, John
17	Laskowske, Libby
18	Murphy, Peter ET UX
19	King, Alida
20	Post, Monroe Jacob ET UX
21	McGrane, Anna May ET AL
22	Murphy, Peter ET UX
23	Hogan, Emma C.
25A	Seeley, Richard Montgomery ET UX
25B	Deady, Laverna
28	Olsowske, Paul ET UX
29	Guilfoos, Harry ET AL
29A	Lehigh Valley Railway Company
30A	Seeley, Richard Montgomery ET UX
31	McGrane, Estate of John, John E. McGrane, Exec.
32	Cook, Clara ET AL

Parcel Number	Name of Property Owner
33	Kreutter, Estate of Albert J., Henry J. Hoster, Exec.
34	O'Marra, Matin ET UX
35	Thompson, Adelbert Abner
37	First National Bank of Waterloo
38	Van Riper, Burt B.
39	Robbins, Harold M. ET UX
40	Covert, Albert J. ET UX
41	Van Riper, Albertus A. ET AL
41A	O'Connor, Emerson G.—Commissioner of Public Welfare Seneca County
44	Van Riper, Jay
45	The Seneca Falls Savings Bank
45A	Thompson, Martha B.
46	Covert, Albert J. ET UX
46A	Moses, Myrtle C.
47	Buchholz, Wilson G.H. ET AL
47A	Trustees of School District No. 19 of Varick
48	Phillips, Chester W. ET AL
49A	Buchholz, Wilson ET AL
50	Keefer, Walter B.
51	Lockwood, Francis H.
51A	Osborne, Thomas W.
51B	The Lehigh Valley Railway Company
53	Campbell, Rosetta
53A	The Varick Wesleyan Methodist Church ET AL
54	Ehle, George G.
55	The Varick Wesleyan Methodist Church ET AL
56	Lisk, John B.
57	Lisk, Edith S.
58	Van Riper, Jay H. ET AL
60	Van Riper, Ernest N. ET UX
61	Lockwood, Francis H.

Parcel Number	Name of Property Owner
62	Thorp, Fred C.
63	Thorpe, Lead E., ET UX
63A	Briggs, Scott ET UX
64	Phillips, Chester W. ET AL
64A	Van Riper, Barton L. ET UX
65	Crane, Martha B.
68	Yates, Violet ET AL
70	Everett, Lillian I.
71	Baldridge, Charles J.
73	Komonek, Frank ET UX
75	White, John T.
76	Lisk, John B. ET AL
77	Deasy, John E.
78	Pettit, Harry ET UX
79	Collins, Albert G. ET UX
80	Jacobus, Charles H.
81	Montford, C. Edward
83	Bolles, Emma S.
83A	O'Marra, William ET UX
84	Walker, E.P.

Note:
ET UX after the name means "and wife (spouse)."
ET AL after the name means "and others."

NOTES

Chapter 1

1. Writings of former Seneca County Historian Betty Auten.
2. *Final Report, Task Order 001 Documentary Research: Seneca Army Depot Activities, Romulus, Seneca County, New York*, September 1998, 7.
3. Ibid., 8.
4. L. Dean Bruno, "Once a Home, Now a Memory: Dispossession, Possession and Remembrance of the Landscape of the Former Seneca Army Depot," master's thesis at North Carolina State University, 13–14.
5. Ibid., 18.
6. Walter Gable, "Early History of Kendaia."
7. Ibid., 18–19.
8. Hilda R. Watrous, *The County Between the Lakes: A History of Seneca County New York 1876–1982*, Waterloo, NY: K-Mar Press, Inc., 1983, 2.
9. Bruno, "Once a Home," 21
10. Walter Gable, "The Military Tract"
11. Bruno, "Once a Home," 28–34.
12. Gable, "The Military Tract," 7.
13. *Final Report*, 14–18.
14. Ibid., 22.
15. Ibid., 22, 26.
16. Ibid., 28.
17. Ibid., 28.
18. Ibid., 30–31.
19. Ibid., 31, 35.
20. Ibid., 36, 39.

Chapter 2

21. http://www.history.army.mil/documents/mobpam.htm
22. Stanley L. Engerman and Robert E. Gallman, *The Cambridge Economic History of the United States: The Twentieth Century*, Cambridge University Press, 2000, 358.
23. Watrous, *County Between the Lakes*, 23.
24. Harry C. Thomson and Linda Mayo, *United States Army in World War II—The Technical Services: The Ordnance Department: Procure and Supply*, Washington, D.C.: Center of Military History, United States Army, 2003, 371.
25. Watrous, *County Between the Lakes*, 23.
26. Editorial, *Waterloo Observer*, July 18, 1941.
27. "Weekly Payroll to Run Over $250,000, Say Army Officers," *Geneva Daily Times*, June 25, 1941.
28. *Syracuse Post-Standard*, May 15, 1941.
29. "Munitions Depot Office Takes on Activity with Arrival of Contractors," *Syracuse Post-Standard*, July 2, 1941.
30. Bruno, "Once a Home," 57.
31. "U.S. Approves Plans For Munitions Depot Road, Rail Network," *Rochester Times-Union*, July 16, 1941.
32. "Recent Doings Altered Time, Officer Says," *Rochester Democrat and Chronicle*, July 31, 1941.
33. Bruno, "Once a Home," 58.
34. Thomson and Mayo, *Army in World War II*, 371.
35. Bruno, "Once a Home," 60–63.
36. Conversation between Walter Gable and Mrs. Charmion Dinsmore on March 6, 2011.
37. "Prompted by Patriotism, Cash, Farmers Leave Bomb-Depot Site," *Buffalo Evening News*, August 2, 1941.

Chapter 3

38. *Syracuse Post-Standard*, July 15, 1941.
39. Bruno, "Once a Home," 64.
40. "Three-Day Notice to Quit Century Old Farm in Depot Area Fails to Dim Lisks' Patriotism," *Syracuse Post Standard*, July 26, 1941.
41. Ibid.
42. Bruno, "Once a Home," 68.
43. Ibid., 59–60.

44. Ibid., 60.
45. Ibid., 64.
46. Florence Vargason, interview, August 15, 2010.
47. Barton VanRiper, private correspondence, July 22, 23, 1941.
48. Bruno, "Once a Home," 68.
49. Ibid., 67
50. *Geneva Daily Times*, September 8, 1941.
51. *Syracuse Herald Journal*, August 29, 1941.
52. *Elmira Telegraph*, August 10, 1941.
53. Ibid.
54. Bruno, "Once a Home," 69, 71.
55. *Geneva Daily Times*, September 8, 1941.
56. *Rochester Democrat and Chronicle*, September 8, 1941.
57. Bruno, "Once a Home," 81.
58. Walter Gable, 2011.
59. Bruno, "Once a Home," 58.
60. Ibid.
61. Ibid., 87.

CHAPTER 4

62. John E. Becker, *A History of the Village of Waterloo, New York and Thesaurus of Related Facts*, Waterloo, NY: Waterloo Library and Historical Society, 1949, 426.
63. Ibid., 426–427.
64. Ibid., 427.
65. Watrous, *County Between the Lakes*, 7.
66. Ibid., 8.
67. "Col. Parker Head of Munition Depot Addresses Legionaires," *Seneca County Press*, July 9, 1941.
68. "Weekly Payroll to Run Over $250,000, Say Army Officers," *Geneva Daily Times*, June 25, 1941.
69. "County Offices Busy As Clerks Aid in Search of Records For Land Transfer," *Geneva Daily Times*, July 11, 1941.
70. Watrous, *County Between the Lakes*, 8.
71. Ibid., 10–11.
72. Ibid., 10.
73. "Weekly Payroll to Run Over $250,000, Say Army Officers," *Geneva Daily Times*, June 25, 1941.
74. "U.S. Sights Added Cost for Depot," *Rochester Democrat and Chronicle*, June 28, 1941.

75. "Weekly Payroll to Run Over $250,000, Say Army Officers," *Geneva Daily Times*, June 25, 1941.
76. "Seneca County Ordnance Depot Job Started Near Kendaia—U.S. Army Officers Are in Charge," *Seneca Falls Reveille*, July 11, 1941.
77. "Kendaia in Initial Throes of Boom Town," *Geneva Daily Times*, July 15, 1941.
78. "Employment Rises In Steady Stream At Ordnance Depot," *Syracuse Post-Standard*, July 16, 1941.
79. "'Pioneers' Are Laboring By Candle-light at Big Seneca Ordnance Depot," *Auburn Citizen-Advertiser*, July 26, 1941.
80. "Kendaia Depot May Become Army, Navy Plane Base," *Geneva Daily Times*, July 15, 1941.
81. Watrous, *County Between the Lakes*, 10.
82. Ibid., 23.
83. Ibid., 23–24.
84. Ibid., 11.
85. "Citizens' Duties Cited At Ceremony," *Rochester Democrat and Chronicle*, August 22, 1941.
86. "Colors Raised At Bomb Reservation, Igloo Takes Shape," *Auburn Citizen-Advertiser*, August 22, 1941.
87. "Kendaia Site Dedicated As Army Depot," *Rochester Democrat and Chronicle*, August 22, 1941.
88. Watrous, *County Between the Lakes*, 10–11.
89. *Ovid Gazette*, August 8, 1941.
90. Watrous, *County Between the Lakes*, 18.
91. Ibid., 11.
92. Ibid., 18.
93. Ibid., 21.
94. "Newspaper Men See Igloos In The Making at Kendaia," *Ovid Gazette*, October 24, 1941.
95. Watrous, *County Between the Lakes*, 21.
96. "Construction of Igloos at Ordnance Depot Nears Completion: 400 Ready For Final Touches," *Rochester Times-Union*, November 3, 1941.
97. "Depot Data," *Geneva Daily Times*, November 15, 1941.
98. Watrous, *County Between the Lakes*, 21.
99. Jack Meddoff, "Concrete Poured Day and Night To Build Bomb Depot by Winter," *Buffalo Evening News*, October 23, 1941.
100. "Small Weather Bureau Is Set Up at Kendaia Depot," *Geneva Daily Times*, November 1, 1941.
101. Watrous, *County Between the Lakes*, 9.

102. Ibid., 10.
103. Ibid., 11.
104. Ibid., 12.
105. Ibid., 14.
106. Ibid., 22.
107. Ibid., 23.
108. Ibid., 23–24.
109. Ibid., 8.
110. Ibid., 11.
111. Ibid., 12–13.
112. "3,472 Registrants From Geneva at Seneca Army Depot," *Geneva Daily Times*, September 6, 1941.
113. "Employment Rises In Steady Stream At Ordnance Depot," *Syracuse Post-Standard*, July 16, 1941.
114. "Genevan Aids Job Seekers," *Rochester Democrat and Chronicle*, July 17, 1941.
115. "Labor on Ordnance Depot Is Declared 80 Per Cent Local," *Syracuse Post-Standard*, September 13, 1941.
116. "Trailer and Tent Dwellers Working in Seneca County Say They Like the Life," *Geneva Daily Times*, September 15, 1941.
117. Comments made on February 9, 2011, by Naomi Brewer, who, with her late husband, Fenton, reported that was true for her lake property as well as others.
118. "Laborer's Families Live in Tents and Trailers at Kendaia," *Syracuse Herald-Journal*, August 25, 1941.
119. Watrous, *County Between the Lakes*, 12.
120. Ibid.
121. Ibid.
122. "Dangers Cited in Worker Influx," *Rochester Times-Union*, September 5, 1941.
123. "Col. Parker Issues Statement on Housing: Says Trailer Camp Problem Is Matter of Enforcing Health Law," *Geneva Daily Times*, September 11, 1941.
124. "Sanitary Conditions at Ordnance Depot Present Grave Dangers, Official Says," *Syracuse Herald-American*, September 14, 1941.
125. Watrous, *County Between the Lakes*, 16.
126. "Conditions at Bomb Depot Declared Like Those 'In Hobo Jungle,'" *Auburn Citizen-Advertiser*, September 13, 1941.
127. Watrous, *County Between the Lakes*, 17.
128. "Congressman Taber Visits Bomb Depot to Get Sanitation Fact," *Auburn Citizen-Advertiser*, September 15, 1941.
129. "Federal and State Action on Ordnance Depot Housing Seen," *Geneva Daily Times*, September 13, 1941.

130. "Lieut. Governor Poletti Sends State Troopers Here-Make Housing Canvass in Two Day," *Seneca Falls Reveille*, September 19, 1941.
131. Ibid.
132. "Report Nearly 1500 Rooms Are Available," *Geneva Daily Times*, September 18, 1941.
133. "Lieut. Governor Poletti Sends State Troopers Here-Make Housing Canvass in Two Day," *Seneca Falls Reveille*, September 19, 1941.
134. "Poletti Taken on Tour of Inspection of Kendaia Depot," *Geneva Daily Times*, September 22, 1941.
135. "Police Survey Housing to Ease Kendaia Plight," *Syracuse Post-Standard*, September 14, 1941.
136. Watrous, *County Between the Lakes*, 19.
137. "Trailers Ordered to Evacuate Land About New Ordnance Depot," *Geneva Daily Times*, October 4, 1941.
138. "Trailer Camp Established At Kendaia," *Syracuse Herald-Journal*, October 5, 1941.
139. "Trailer Edict Meets With Strong Protest," *Geneva Daily Times*, October 9, 1941.
140. Becker, *Village of Waterloo*, 427–28.
141. Watrous, *County Between the Lakes*, 20–21.
142. Ibid., 25–26.
143. Ibid., 26.
144. Ibid., 11.
145. "Depot Strike Ends As Men Get Raise," *Waterloo Observer*, September 19, 1941.
146. "Highway Heads Hear of Depot Progress," *Rochester Democrat and Chronicle*, September 20, 1941.
147. "Kendaia Drivers Halt Trucks Until Assured Increase," *Syracuse Post-Standard*, October 2, 1941.
148. "Tiny Kendaia Blossoming As Big Boon Town," *Auburn Citizen-Advertizer*, July 12, 1941.
149. "Kendaia Bustling As Shovels Clear Wide Depot Area," *Syracuse Post-Standard*, 7-20-1941.
150. "Kendaia in Initial Throes of Boom Town," *Geneva Daily Times*, July 15, 1941.
151. "Concrete Igloos For Bombs Built At Finger Lakes," *Syracuse Herald-Journal*, August 12, 1941.
152. "Kendaia General Store Business Increases By 400 P.C. Due to New Ordnance Depot," *Syracuse Herald-Journal*, September 6, 1941.
153. "Romulus Becomes Boom Town as Workers Flock to Ammunition Depot Job," *Syracuse Herald-Journal*, October 1, 1941.

154. "Geneva Finds Retail Trade At New Peaks," *Rochester Democrat and Chronicle*, October 19, 1941.
155. "Geneva Business Booms With Big Ordnance Depot as Vital Factor," *Geneva Daily Times*, October 13, 1941.
156. "2 Shifts to begin Work Today on Kendaia Project," *Syracuse Post-Standard*, July 28, 1941.
157. Watrous, *County Between the Lakes*, 11.
158. "Kendaia in Initial Throes of Boom Town," *Geneva Daily Times*, July 15, 1941.
159. "Jail Houses Workers From Depot," *Rochester Democrat and Chronicle*, October 2, 1941.
160. "Jordan Brothers Colorful Quartet of Construction of Ordnance Depot," *Syracuse Post-Standard*, October 5, 1941.
161. "Mrs. Roosevelt Asks FR to Rush Delivery of Seneca Trailers," *Syracuse Post-Standard*, October 1, 1941.
162. "Mrs. Roosevelt Cuts Red Tape to Speed Housing," *New York-Herald Tribune*, October 1, 1941.
163. "Depot Data," *Geneva Daily Times*, November 25, 1941.
164. "Depot Data," *Geneva Daily Times*, November 30, 1941.
165. http://www.globalsecurity.org/military/facility/seneca.htm
166. August 1942 local newspaper article.
167. http://www.globalsecurity.org/military/facility/seneca.htm

CHAPTER 5

168. Watrous, *County Between the Lakes*, 25.
169. Foreword to some informational publication given to depot workers at some point during the war.
170. "New Instructions On Operations Received At Ordnance," *Seneca Falls Reveille*, July 23, 1943.
171. *Syracuse Herald-Journal*, March 31, 1943.
172. Arthur Wood, Gannett Newspapers, April 6, 1943
173. http://globalsecurity.org/military/facility/seneca.htm.
174. Roger Allerton telephone interview, April 3, 2011.
175. Elizabeth Harding interview, March 9, 2011.
176. Roger Allerton telephone interview, April 3, 2011.
177. *Seneca Falls Reveille*, March 26, 1943.
178. Information told by Eva Scarrott to Walter Gable many years ago.
179. *Syracuse Post-Standard*, August 6, 1944.
180. Roger Allerton telephone interview, March 31, 2011.

181. Glenn White telephone interview, March 23, 2011.
182. Elizabeth Harding interview, March 9, 2011.
183. http://www.rootsweb,ancestry.com/~txrober2/TissingI.htm.
184. http://www.prisonersinparadise.com/history.html.
185. "Local Men Form Sunday Work Group To Speed Shipments At Ordnance Depot," *Seneca County Press*, February 14, 1943.
186. "Congressman Taber To Speak At Depot Flag Raising Monday," *Seneca Falls Reveille*, May 28, 1943.
187. "Ordnance Bomb Explosions Cause Anxiety Here," *Seneca Falls Reveille*, April 20, 1945.
188. "Seneca Depot," *Rochester Democrat and Chronicle*, August 2, 1983.
189. http://en.wikipedia.org/wiki/Seneca_Army_Depot.
190. Interview of John Stahl conducted by Walter Gable conducted on March 8, 2011.
191. "Seneca Army Depot will be 28 years old tomorrow," *Geneva Times*, August 8, 1969.

Chapter 6

192. Watrous, *County Between the Lakes*, 29–30.
193. http://www.globalsecurity.org/military/facility/seneca.htm.
194. http://www.globalsecurity.org/military/facility/seneca.htm.
195. "Depot Salute," *Finger Lakes Times*, August 7, 1991.
196. Watrous, *County Between the Lakes*, 30.
197. "Seneca Army Depot was born 29 years ago," *Geneva Times*, August 8, 1970.
198. "Depot Salute," *Finger Lakes Times*, August 7, 1991, 2A.
199. "Depot Salute," *Finger Lakes Times*, 8-7-1991, 5A.
200. "Seneca Army Depot was born 29 years ago," *Geneva Times*, August 8, 1970.
201. "Depot Salute," *Finger Lakes Times*, August 7, 1991, 3A.
202. Watrous, *County Between the Lakes*, 30.
203. "Seneca Army Depot was born 29 years ago," *Geneva Times*, August 8, 1970.
204. "Depot Salute," *Finger Lakes Times*, August 7, 1991.
205. www.senecawhitedeer.org/white-deer-natural-resources/white-deeer-seneca-army-depot/.
206. Walter Gable, "Seneca Army Depot—Then and Now," article written as Seneca County Historian making use of various sources of information. This article can be accessed on the Seneca County website www.co.seneca.ny.us.

207. Bill Delancey, "Outdoor Chatter," *Geneva Daily Times*, November 17, 1954.
208. http://www.senecawhitedeer.org/about/our-mission/.
209. Gable, "Seneca Army Depot—Then and Now."
210. Information supplied by Pat Jones, Deputy Executive Director, Seneca County IDA, April 6, 2011.

CHAPTER 7

211. http://dmna.state.ny.us/fortsQ_S/senecaArmyDepot/htm.
212. Gable, "Seneca Army Depot—Then and Now."
213. Mark Hare, "Our own doomsday machine," *City Newspaper*, October 15, 1981.
214. Ibid.
215. Ibid. All of the "bulleted" pieces of evidence mentioned to this point come from this source.
216. "Seneca Depot," *Rochester Democrat and Chronicle*, August 2, 1983.
217. Interview of Robert Zemanek by Walter Gable on March 18, 2011. Mr. Zemanek was the Public Affairs Officer at the depot from December 1972 until his retirement in 1990. These last two bulleted pieces of evidence come from this interview.
218. "Seneca Depot," *Rochester Democrat and Chronicle*, August 2, 1983.
219. Mark Hare, "Our own doomsday machine," *City Newspaper*, October 15, 1981.
220. "Seneca Depot," *Rochester Democrat and Chronicle*, August 2, 1983.
221. http://en.wikipedia.org/wiki/The_Seneca_Women's_Encampment_for_a_Future_of_Peace.
222. Ibid.
223. Ibid.
224. *Finger Lakes Times*, August 4, 1983.
225. http://wikimapia.org/16264093/Seneca-Army-Depot-Former.
226. *Southeast Missourian*, October 25, 1983
227. Ibid.
228. *Finger Lakes Times*, July 13, 1985.

CHAPTER 8

229. Information taken from interview of Bernard Hauf and Michael Lambert on August 7, 2012.
230. Information presented from interviews of Bruce Johnson, Michael Lambert, Bev Lombardo and Bernard Hauf.

231. Susan Clark Porter, "Army Depot Closing Final," *Finger Lakes Times*, July 21, 2000.
232. Ibid.
233. http://cfpub.epa.gov/supercpad/cursites/csitinfor.cfm?id=0202425.

Chapter 9

234. http://www.senecacountyida.org/about.
235. http://www.senecacountryida.org/sie/contact_list.
236. http://www.senecacountyida.org/about/board_members.
237. http://cfpub.epa.gov/supercpad/cursites/csitinfo.cfm?id=0202425.
238. http://www.senecacountyida.org/site/case_studies/finger-lakes-technolgoies-group-inc.
239. "Soldiers to train at former Army depot," *Finger Lakes Times*, March 17, 2011.
240. *Manual of the Churches of Seneca County with Sketches of Their Pastors, 1895–96*, Seneca Falls, NY: Courier Printing Company, 1896, 65–67.
241. Bruno, "Once a Home," 77–79.
242. Schuyler County Historian Barbara H. Bell letter in 2011 to Seneca County Historian Walter Gable.

Appendix II

243. Timeline prepared by Seneca County Historian Walter Gable, revised February 2011.

Appendix III

244. *Inactivation Ceremony: Relinquishment of Command, 20 July 2000* pamphlet.

INDEX

I

J

K

L

M

T

U

V

W

Y

Z

ABOUT THE AUTHORS

Walter Gable

Walter Gable has been the Seneca County Historian since August 2003. A lifelong resident of Seneca County, he is a graduate of the Romulus Central School District and earned his bachelor's and master's degrees at Syracuse University. He taught high school social studies for thirty years at Mynderse Academy in the Seneca Falls Central School District. He was president of the New York State Council for Social Studies (1997–98) and recognized as Distinguished Social Studies Educator in New York State in 2000. Walt credits his lifelong interest in history to his enthusiastic high school history teacher, Ethel Buckley.

Carolyn Zogg

After retiring as a national nonprofit director, Ms. Zogg was appointed director of the Seneca Falls Historical Society and its Becker House Museum. She served on the board of directors for Celebrate '98, which commemorated 150 years of the women's rights movement, which originated in Seneca Falls in 1848. In 1999, she successfully received national historical accreditation for Lodi Historical Society's Hook Opus 152 tracker organ, built 1852. Carolyn is past president and Trustee Emerita of the Lodi Historical Society. A graduate of Syracuse University, Zogg received her provisional teaching certificate from the State University of New York at New Paltz, New York, in art education. She lives on Seneca Lake at Lodi Point, where her family has summered since 1935. Carolyn is known in her community for her savory deviled eggs and old-fashioned bread-and-butter pickles.